"Upon reading *lifeFocus: Achieving a Life of Purpose and Influence*, one is struck with the knowledge that this is an innovative, broad life-planning approach few people have attempted or purposefully used. It encourages readers to consider a new way of approaching a life plan.

"Opportunities to exceed one's own expectation for a life's journey toward success will be enhanced many times over by utilizing the principles described so thoughtfully in this book. It is an easy read full of applicable real-life examples that broaden and underscore the key points.

"Developing life plans that include all dimensions of wealth—financial, relational, physical, spiritual, and intellectual—is the best, perhaps the only way to fulfill our dreams of living a life that provides fulfillment and satisfaction."

—MARY KRAMER, UNITED STATES AMBASSADOR TO BARBADOS

"Common sense and biblical wisdom are becoming increasingly rare. Yet you will find both of those valuable commodities oozing off every page of *lifeFocus*."

—STEVE FARRAR, MEN'S LEADERSHIP MINISTRIES

"In *lifeFocus* Jerry Foster defines true personal wealth and exhorts us to follow principles and practices to attain this life wealth. The people in our lives will be blessed and God will be honored by our building this type of personal wealth. I urge you to read this book, apply it to your life, and share it with others."

—CAL ELDRED, MAJOR LEAGUE BASEBALL PLAYER

"*LifeFocus* is a breath of fresh air! My husband and I learned that small changes now in the allocation of our time, energy, and resources can yield big results in the long run."

—JENEE PETERSON, HOMEMAKER

"God created each of us with great potential, but it's the big and small choices we make each day that determine whether our lives are fulfilling or empty. As you read Jerry's book you will gain insights into how you can make every area of your life the most fulfilling and live life to the fullest. Read this book—it'll equip you for life!"

—DENNIS AND BARBARA RAINEY, COFOUNDERS OF FAMILYLIFE

"Jerry Foster has painted a vivid image of the paths of indulgence, indifference, and influence that we all, either consciously or unconsciously, choose. His concept of small vector changes now creating huge differences later is very powerful. Jerry creates not only the inspiration but a practical way of implementing life-changing decisions."

—MIKE DAVIS, PRESIDENT, RESOURCE CONSULTING GROUP

"Implementing these concepts has helped bring order to the chaos of our busy lives. I highly recommend this book to people struggling with balance in their lives."

—MIKE ABRAMS, EXECUTIVE VICE PRESIDENT, IOWA MEDICAL SOCIETY *life*Focus

*life*Focus

ACHIEVING A LIFE OF PURPOSE
AND INFLUENCE

Jerry Foster
with Ed Stewart

Revell
Grand Rapids, Michigan

© 2004 by Jerry Foster

Published by Fleming H. Revell
a division of Baker Book House Company
P.O. Box 6287, Grand Rapids, MI 49516-6287
www.bakerbooks.com

Published in association with the literary agency of Alive Communications, Inc., 7680 Goddard Street, Suite 200, Colorado Springs, Colorado, 80920.

Printed in the United States of America

Library of Congress Cataloging-in-Publication Data
Foster, Jerry, 1955–
    Lifefocus: achieving a life of purpose and influence / Jerry Foster
with Ed Stewart.
            p.   cm.
    Includes bibliographical references.
    ISBN 0-8007-5959-1 (pbk.)
    1. Success—Religious aspects—Christianity. I. Stewart, Ed. II.
Title.
BV4598.3.F67 2004
158—dc22   2003027481

To my wife, Nancy, who has come alongside me
as my encourager, completer, and biggest cheerleader!
You are indeed my life partner and soul mate.

To my children,
Brooke, Ryan, Angie, Regan, and Kaity,
who have become my legacy
and give me reason every day to give it my all.
I am so proud of you!

Contents

———————•———————

Acknowledgments

———————•———————

Wealthy is the person who has many friends who are cheerleaders, faithful coworkers who are dependable, wise gatekeepers who open doors, and a loving family who is supportive no matter what. This book is complete because of the many friends and key players who gave of their time and talents. I want to thank them for motivating, encouraging, challenging, and touching my life in so many ways.

To our good friends Mike and Linda Colby: You have been there for Nancy and me so many years, and we know we can count on you as we finish life side by side. Thanks for being my cheerleaders. What more could we want than friends who demonstrate unconditional love?

To my friend and accountability partner Gary Rosberg: You and Barb have led by example, and your faithfulness has been an inspiration to me. You went the extra mile to open doors for me, and for that I am forever grateful. It is an honor to walk through life with you.

To Ed Stewart, who contributed so much to this manuscript: You are truly a wordsmith and have found your niche. I don't know where I even would have begun without you.

To the team at Baker Book House: Thank you for the opportunity to write about what has been on my heart for years. The confidence you have placed in me is an incredible encouragement. A special thanks to Vicki Crumpton—you challenged me to another level of writing as we passed the manuscript back and forth too many times to count.

To the team at Foster Group: There is no finer team in America. Your professionalism, integrity, competence, and loyalty has given me the peace of mind and confidence to commit the necessary time to this important project.

To my parents, Jerry and Pat Foster, who faithfully modeled for me what it looks like to finish well: As you retired from your vocations, you invested in your avocation, serving others and building your legacy.

Finally, to Nancy, Brooke, Ryan, Angie, Regan, Kaity, and Luis: You are the joy of my life, the inspiration behind this book. You have been the recipients of many of my mistakes and failures that became learning experiences upon which I have drawn while encouraging others. Thank you for your patience and tolerance. You are my heroes!

Foreword

_____•_____

One of the greatest joys in my life is watching the transformation that takes place when a person moves from the pursuit of success to the pursuit of significance. I personally went through that transformation and recounted my experience in my first book, *Halftime*. As you will read in the pages of this book, Jerry reached a point in his life where he too was asking himself how he wanted to spend the rest of his life. Wherever you are, this book will help you answer that question too.

Jerry has painted a vivid image of the paths we spend most of our lives on. As Jerry shares, we will make a choice, either consciously or unconsciously, to live a life of indifference, indulgence, or influence. Our choice will have significant impact on the fulfillment and satisfaction we have in our lives. Our choice will also have lasting impact on those we love and generations to come.

I have never met a person who didn't want to influence others in some capacity. We were all created for a purpose, and all given spheres of influence where we can exercise our gifts and live our lives to the fullest potential. The problem is that the day-to-day grind and pressures of life crowd out the pursuit of that dream and we become lost in the minutia of life and the tyranny of the urgent. We get off the path of influence.

If you can identify with some of these thoughts, then I am confident this book will motivate, encourage, and challenge you to find the formula for balancing your life and dreaming of what could be in the world around you. Jerry's concept of small changes that you can make now, creating huge differences later, is very powerful. He creates not only the inspiration, but a practical way of implementing life-changing decisions.

My encouragement to you is to take this book, use the questions for thought and discussion, and accept Jerry's challenge in each chapter to change your life one step at a time. If you will do that, then you will be well on your way to experiencing the joy of a fulfilling life and will have the tools necessary to achieve a life of purpose and influence.

Bob Buford
Author of *Halftime*
Founder of Leadership Network

1

How to Get Where You Want to Go

———————•———————

How do you want your life to end? With your final breath do you want to utter, "What a satisfying, fulfilling, and meaningful life I have lived"? Do you desire your relationship with your spouse and children to grow closer and stronger right to the very end? Do you want to leave a rich legacy of material *and* nonmaterial treasures for your heirs? Do you hope that friends and coworkers who attend your memorial service are filled with gratitude for your contribution to their lives? I don't know a single person who wouldn't give anything to finish in such a way.

So here's the rubber-meets-the-road question: Do you know how to get *there* from *here*? Are you headed toward a positive outcome in your daily, weekly, and monthly choices, or are your values and priorities veering you off in another direction? You definitely can get *there* (the life you really want) from *here* (the life you presently lead) when you apply the principle that small changes can make a big difference over the course of your life.

Vector, a term in mathematics and physics, quantifies the speed and direction of an object. If you were the pilot of a jetliner, you would use vectors to define the course to your destination. When you are given a new vector by the control center, you turn the plane to line up with that heading on the compass, creating a new vector angle.

Obviously, even the smallest vector change in the cockpit can make a big difference in the plane's ultimate destination. Though it may seem an imperceptible change, with every mile traveled you are farther from your previous course. For example, you could make a tiny vector change while flying between New York and Seattle and end up in Los Angeles instead. Some vectors require a drastic change of direction, such as taking off to the west and vectoring 180 degrees for an eastbound flight. However, most flights are achieved through a series of rather small vectors, minor turns and course adjustments that allow the cockpit crew to fly the plane from point A to point B.

The Vector Principle applies to our lives in the same manner. Even if you never fly an airplane, you are vectoring through life by the choices you make. You are currently on a course that was determined by choices you have made since you were aware of your capacity to choose. Many of these choices seemed rather insignificant at the time, but small changes make a big difference over time.

I am absolutely convinced that this principle will take you where you want to go. How can I be so sure? My wife and I have lived the Vector Principle for the past twenty-plus years and are today experiencing the fruit of the vector changes we have made. Here's our story.

16

Changing Course

We'd had another tense and tearful evening at home. As was often the case, the snipping started over my insensitivity. I had brought home a bunch of buddies from my softball team after a game, expecting my wife to be ready with cookies and lemonade for everyone. But Nancy didn't have anything ready because I hadn't said a word about the guys coming over or about refreshments. Her displeasure at a surprise visit by a bunch of sweaty ball players was obvious.

"Why can't you be nice to my friends?" I demanded when we were alone.

Nancy fired back, "Why is my life always about adjusting to what you want in your life? What am I—the maid? Do you bring your buddies home just to show them how I can trot out the cookies on command?"

"Look, is it too much to ask for a few cookies and drinks for my friends?" I asked not too kindly.

"I'm not your mom!" Nancy exploded.

The familiar argument blazed hotter from there. When we married a few years earlier, we settled in my hometown where Nancy knew no one. We both worked full-time, but Nancy came home after work and took care of most of the household jobs. I revisited my preuniversity lifestyle—hanging out with friends, joining old softball and basketball teams, and leaving my wife home alone to do most of the work. On one occasion I took Nancy to a party, only to desert her at the door while I went to talk with my friends. My ongoing lack of attentiveness soon prompted bitterness and anger in Nancy.

Tonight's clash quickly spread to other areas of conflict. I chipped at Nancy about the household chores. Nancy railed on me for my irresponsibility with finances. Then at bedtime the fiery exchanges turned stone cold. We climbed into bed and switched off the light without saying goodnight, immediately turning back-to-back, hugging our respective sides of the bed.

Lying in the darkness, I pondered how my dream marriage had become a nightmare in less than three years. Feelings of love had been overcome by frustration, friction, and anger bordering on hatred. *What have I gotten myself into? Is this the way it's always going to be with her? I can't go on like this. What am I going to do?*

Nancy's constant nagging about my independent lifestyle was getting on my nerves. And our finances were a disaster—bounced checks, maxed-out credit card, zero savings, past-due bills—giving us even more to fight about. Since I was just starting my career, I wasn't making much money. And I didn't really enjoy what I was doing. I wasn't using my talents, and I felt trapped. My whole life seemed to be going flat all at once, and I wished I could trade it in and start over. I had to do something.

Meanwhile, on the other side of the bed, tears rolled down Nancy's face onto the pillow. My lack of sensitivity and leadership in the home left Nancy feeling betrayed, abandoned, and scared.

The wall of isolation between us grew taller and wider. As I poured more of my time into my friends and unfulfilling career, Nancy became less attentive to me. We were already in trouble financially, and I wasn't doing anything about it. Trying to balance the checkbook every month left her in a panic.

This isn't the man I thought I was marrying, Nancy thought. *He only thinks about himself; he's not interested in me or my needs. He's spending us into the poorhouse. He hates his job. What if he gets fired? We could lose the house. I can't stand this kind of pressure. It would be different if he really loved me and was concerned about me, but I sure don't feel it. And I've lost any feeling of love for him. I wonder if this marriage was meant to be.*

A few weeks later, one of Nancy's coworkers invited her to join a study group on how to renew love in your marriage. Her first thought was that her marriage was beyond hope. Attending the group seemed like such a tiny step toward solving a huge problem. But what did she have to lose? So she joined the group.

Nancy's eyes were opened as she met other women who struggled with the same concerns in their marriages. In the group she learned how to encourage her husband, esteem him, and pray for him instead of nagging at him. Since the nagging and yelling hadn't worked, she decided to try a positive approach.

The first thing Nancy noticed was a gradual change in her own attitude and feelings toward me. She was less critical and more sympathetic than she had been. Her new attitude had an effect on me too. When I came home from work one day, I said to Nancy, "I heard about a seminar on finances being held next weekend. It's supposed to help people organize their money. Do you want to go . . . I mean, together?"

Nancy wanted to be encouraging, but she was skeptical. "We can't afford to go to a seminar."

"The way things are," I said almost apologetically, "maybe we can't afford *not* to go."

So we went to the seminar. Much of the content was either over our heads or unrealistic for our situation. But we did come away with one simple idea. We had to work through a few arguments to get it done, but we finally agreed on a bare-bones monthly budget. Attacking our financial problems together brought us closer. Nancy noticed that I worked hard to make the budget succeed. Little by little she began to trust me with our finances.

In the midst of our slow progress, we took another small, positive step together. We decided to attend a local conference on building healthy marriages. Again we came away from the conference with one simple idea for improving our marriage. We joined a small group of couples in the community who sought to grow harmonious, positive marriage relationships. We began to bond with some new friends who were also dealing with incompatibility, money issues, parenting, and various areas of conflict. Whenever we picked up a helpful strategy, we tried it out. Step by step, decision by decision, strategy by strategy, our love was rekindled and our lives grew in fulfillment.

With things progressing on the home front, I attended a class at a local university to help me identify my strengths and interests for building a fulfilling career. I realized I had a lot to offer the business world. I began to use skills I never knew I possessed. I gained confidence in myself, and Nancy began to see a difference in my ability to take responsibility at home.

The twenty-plus years since that time have seen continuous growth in our lives and marriage. We followed these simple, early baby steps of progress, along with many others, in the areas of finances, marriage relationship, friendships, and career. Good things happened. Though all wasn't sweetness and light—we still had misunderstandings, mistakes, and arguments—most of the time our conflicts ended with a positive step to remedy the problem.

As we continued to hone our marriage skills in the support group, we fell in love all over again, and our relationship began to flourish. We continued to attend marriage enrichment conferences and apply what we learned step-by-step. Eventually we became the leaders of a similar group of couples, and for the last several years we have been speakers at the same conference that nudged our marriage in the right direction more than twenty years ago. We are still close friends with many from that first support group, and we have had the privilege of encouraging others in their marriages.

Our attention to sound financial principles brought stability to our income and spending. As we became more stable financially, I made a career change and eventually started a successful business that has afforded us increasing levels of financial freedom. Our financial stability, in turn, allowed us to devote more of our time to volunteer activities.

We recently celebrated twenty-five years of marriage. We aren't the perfect couple, and we don't have it all together. But we are light-years from where we started. We still fine-tune all areas of our life—marriage and family, finances, health and recreation, career, friendships, faith—one step at a time. We learned long ago that most successful people rarely get where they want to go by radical 90- or 180-degree changes. Rather, they take one simple step after another in the right direction, make minor course adjustments over time, institute small changes, and follow a series of less-than-earth-shattering decisions. And it all starts with a few small choices made in the right direction.

You Can Get There from Here

The Vector Principle states, *Achieving a desired outcome in your life is the result of consistently making positive choices that vector you toward that outcome.* In other words, if you want a happy, fulfilling, lifelong marriage, you must consistently make choices that contribute to such a marriage. The same goes for your finances, career, health, other relationships, and faith. Yes, you may need to make a few sharp turns along the way to chart a course toward your life vision, such as a major career change, a move across the country, or a choice regarding faith in God. But most of your vectoring will occur as small adjustments to keep you on course.

The Vector Principle changed our lives, and it has changed the lives of many others we have taught and coached over the years. We have discovered that small adjustments grow into significant transformations over time. More specifically, we have personally experienced the transformation from a life of struggle, dissatisfaction, and despair to one of fulfillment and significance. In the terminology we like to use, we have discovered how to vector our lives to achieve true personal wealth—which we call lifeWealth.

This book is about helping you get from here to there—from whatever state of struggle or emptiness you are experiencing to a life of true personal wealth. It doesn't matter if you are twentysomething and just starting out, fortysomething and well down the road, or sixtysomething and closer to the finish line. It is never too early or too late to vector toward a life of true personal wealth. Here is the course we will take.

Some of the most formidable roadblocks to true personal wealth are the myths about success and fulfillment that are widely accepted as truth in our culture. In part 1 we will explode the myths and misconceptions that may have stalled your progress on the road to true personal wealth.

In order to get from where you are to where you want to be, you must see the big picture. You need a wide-angle, aerial overview of the path to true personal wealth—and the paths that *won't* get you there. In part 2 we will demonstrate how applying the Vector Principle over the long haul will get you where you want to go in life.

Understanding the big picture is vitally important, but we live day to day. True personal wealth is achieved as we vector through life's opportunities and challenges one at a time. In part 3 we will equip you with proven strategies for moving steadily into a life of true personal wealth.

If this is what you want in your life, then join me as we begin this journey to discovering your path to a fulfilling life.

Small Change *Challenges*

- Think about your life story. Make a list of small vector changes that changed the course of your life.
- In a sentence, what is a course change that you would like to make at this point in your life?

Part 1

Myths about True Personal Wealth

2

How Do You Define Success?

———————————•———————————

Joseph Bowen, forty-two, is a highly respected surgeon in his community. After fourteen years in practice, Joe's annual income is comfortably into six figures. Early in his career, he wisely sought counsel from a professional financial planner who helped him devise a strategy for asset management: spending, saving, and investing. Joe worked his financial plan with the same precision he performs surgery, and it has paid off big-time. Joe and his wife, Karen, a part-time critical-care nurse, own a big house in the country, drive new cars, and travel abroad three to four weeks a year. In addition, Joe has a garage full of "toys": boat, motorcycle, snowmobiles, woodworking tools. The surgeon's financial portfolio will allow him to put his two kids through college and retire at fifty-five without sacrificing his comfortable lifestyle. Joe's younger colleagues envy his success.

His colleagues, however, don't know that Joe and Karen have been separated for five months, and the prospects of reconciliation don't look good. Joe has leased a condo in town where he occasionally entertains a new female friend. Furthermore, Joe is getting bored with surgery and fears he is losing his edge. He has talked to his financial team about retiring early—within five years—so he can build wood furniture and travel the world with his girlfriend. But the prospect of a costly divorce, alimony, and child support keeps him in his surgical practice just to stay ahead. Joe doesn't feel very successful.

⋅⋅⋅⋄⋅⋅⋅

The first thing you will notice about Margaret Corelli is her drive. This never-married thirty-six-year-old supervolunteer can't sit still for a minute; she always has to be involved in something big and important. A home-based mail-order business nets Maggie a modest income. But she diverts most of her energy into a growing number of community, environmental, and church activities for which she refuses remuneration. Maggie spends the lion's share of her week chairing committees, spearheading fund-raisers, rescuing wetlands and rare birds, and mobilizing and inspiring numbers of other volunteers who look to her as a hero. Corelli has been voted Outstanding Citizen in her community four years in a row, an honor she relishes.

If you look closely, however, you'll notice something else about Maggie—her sad eyes. Inside this whirling dervish of a volunteer is a lonely woman. In her most candid moments she will tell you that she longs to be married, raise children, and have a few close friends. Maggie is not unattractive or antisocial. Men ask her out occasionally, and many people admire her. But getting close to Maggie is like trying to hop aboard a runaway train. Her drive and

28

busyness push people away. She would gladly trade her Outstanding Citizen awards for relational intimacy, but she doesn't know how.

❖

Don't tell his boss, but twenty-eight-year-old Gabe Dresser would work for nothing. He gets his buzz from the prestige and perks of climbing the corporate ladder in the headquarters of a national insurance firm. Joining the company right out of business college, Gabe threw himself into work. Nobody arrives at the office earlier, stays later, or works more weekends. He has already earned two fairly significant promotions, each coming with the prizes Gabe lives for: a slightly larger office (in his case, still a cubicle), a parking space closer to the front door, new business cards with an impressive new title, his photo and bio in the company newsletter, the applause of his superiors, and the envy of his peers.

But Gabe isn't one to sit on his laurels. His sights are aimed right at the top. His goal is the corner suite on the executive floor—the one occupied by the president of the company—by the time he is forty. And he is willing to give up everything to reach that goal.

Sadly, Gabe's wife, Kitty, and their two preschool-aged sons are already being plowed under in his pursuit. He spends so little time at home that they hardly know him. He promises his family it will all be worth it when he hits the top. This young executive's once-vibrant faith in God and service to his church are also casualties of his quest for position, prestige, and recognition. He spends Sunday mornings at Starbucks reading the trades and gearing up for another winning week at the office. Gabe's steamroller style has also made him a few enemies in the company, coworkers who actively conspire to sabotage his drive to the top. He is the unwitting candidate for a potentially very bad day—being demoted or fired, then coming home deflated to find that Kitty and the boys have moved out.

The Downside of Success

Like Joe, Maggie, and Gabe, everybody wants to experience success at some level. With success as the desired outcome, we make certain decisions that we believe will vector us in that direction. But success means different things to different people. When Joe Bowen launched into his medical career, he vectored toward success by accumulating money and all the pleasurable things it could get him. The financial services industry fosters a lot of people like Joe for whom a bulging asset portfolio is the epitome of success.

Others embracing this financial definition of success don't always yearn to be as wealthy as Joe. Their idea of success may be simply earning enough money to pay all the bills or to buy a new car every four years or to have a savings balance of at least a thousand dollars or to eat at a restaurant once a week or to take a Caribbean cruise. The *amount* of money is relative, determined by one's circumstances and perception of success in financial terms.

Maggie equates success with achievement—in her case, doing good things for the community. The more she accomplishes, the more successful she feels. A lot of people measure success by achievement. They are driven to work harder, faster, and smarter; log more hours; and sacrifice other pleasures and values in order to snag that elusive golden ring of success by getting things done. They are determined to make their mark and make a difference—or die trying. Once again, the *level* or *type* of successful achievement is relative. Your neighbor's lofty view of success may

30

be to rid the community of adult bookstores, while the ultimate in achievement for you may be getting your kids to clean up their rooms without being nagged.

Prestige is another hallmark of success for many people today. Gabe is a good example. The more he is recognized, promoted, and applauded at the insurance company, the more successful he feels. These people live for titles, perks, attention, and a higher rung on the ladder. The ultimate in prestige varies from person to person. Your drive to become chairperson of the local PTA or a church committee is no less important to you than a politician's commitment to become president of the United States, or a struggling actor's desire to land a movie role, or a mountain climber's determination to reach the summit of Mount Everest.

Success has other definitions in our driven culture. The Joes, Maggies, and Gabes of this world live and work next to others who believe success is experienced through fame, power, or happiness—in whatever way those values may be defined. And all these categories of success overlap. Let's be honest here: For most people today, the ultimate in success is to have it all! We look at the millionaires and billionaires of industry, entertainment, and sports and say, "Life doesn't get any better than that." Or we fantasize about winning the $150 million lottery, convinced it will bring us the things, influence, happiness, and contentment we associate with success.

There are many ways by which people across all categories of gender, age, socioeconomic status, and marital status vector toward success in our culture. Yet, as illustrated by these three individuals, many success-driven people arrive at their destination disillusioned and unfulfilled. We see it in the media frequently. Outwardly successful individuals—the rich, the famous, the powerful—become alcoholics or drug addicts, have affairs and destroy their marriages, get involved in crime, or commit suicide. Vectoring toward success doesn't automatically lead to a life of fulfillment and deep satisfaction.

Still, people keep reaching for the elusive gold ring. Why? Because success by most cultural definitions is like a drug. Once you experience the high, it soon wears off and you have to go higher. You get a nice raise to $40K a year, then envy the coworker who makes $47K. You climb Mount Everest for the first time, then have to do it again or succeed from a more difficult approach. Success, that carrot of ultimate fulfillment and satisfaction, while seeming so attainable, always remains just beyond our grasp.

Take money and material possessions, for example. Whatever our income level, it never seems to be enough. We want a bigger TV, a faster computer, a home in a nicer neighborhood, a newer car. And since the bar of affluence is constantly being raised (they are always making things bigger, faster, nicer, and newer!), financial and material success remains a moving target.

In our industry we deal with people whom others would label very successful. Many of them earn excellent money, reaching and exceeding their financial goals. Yet when you talk to these people, a surprising number of them tell you they lack the satisfaction and fulfillment they thought wealth would bring them. They say things such as, "I have all the stuff I want. Why am I not happy? Is this all there is to life?" For them, success—at least their definition of success—isn't all it's cracked up to be.

The same can be true of the other hallmarks of success in our culture. You can climb to the top rung of every ladder—achievement, fame, prestige, power, wealth—and still not feel happy and fulfilled. So if "success" leaves us empty and searching, have we really succeeded? In the words of a Japanese proverb, "He is poor who does not feel content." The dilemma of success without satisfaction challenges us to take a long, hard look at our culture's definition of success.

The Myth of Having More

At the root of the world's view of success is the insatiable quest for more. Another popular word describes the target of this quest—*affluence*. Affluence is defined as "an abundant flow or supply."[1] Notice that affluence isn't limited to "stuff"; it can refer to an abundance of anything. What we have may be good, but more is always viewed as better.

Take power, for example, an icon of success, particularly in the corporate world. In his national best-seller *The 48 Laws of Power,* Robert Greene lays out an incredible approach to acquiring power and wealth at all costs. Here is just a sampling:

Law 2: *Never put too much trust in friends; learn how to use enemies.* Be wary of friends—they will betray you more quickly, for they are easily aroused to envy. If you have no enemies, find a way to make them.

Law 3: *Conceal your intentions.* Keep people off balance and in the dark by never revealing the purpose behind your actions.

Law 11: *Learn to keep people dependent on you.* Make people depend on you for their happiness and prosperity and you have nothing to fear. Never teach them enough that they can do without you.

Law 15: *Crush your enemy totally.* More is lost through stopping halfway than through total annihilation. Crush him, not only in body but in spirit.

Law 33: *Discover each man's thumbscrew.* Everyone has a weakness, a gap in the castle wall. That weakness is usually an insecurity, an uncontrollable emotion or need; it can also be a small pleasure. Either way, once found, it is a thumbscrew you can turn to your advantage.[2]

Would you feel good about the success you achieved and the wealth you accumulated if you achieved them by these standards? Sadly, Greene's laws are the "rules of engagement" for much of our culture today.

We hear the old adages—"Money can't buy happiness" and "It's lonely at the top"—but the seductive message beamed from our TV screens insists that the right possession or position or experience can at least make us happier and more fulfilled than we are. Is this message really true? Apparently not. *The New York Times on the Web* reports that scientific research is revealing a sober reality about the pursuit of affluence:

> Over the last few years . . . psychological researchers have been amassing an impressive body of data suggesting that satisfaction simply is not for sale. Not only does having more things prove to be unfulfilling, but people for whom affluence is a priority in life tend to experience an unusual degree of anxiety and depression as well as lower overall level of well-being.
>
> Likewise, those who would like nothing more than to be famous or attractive do not fare as well, psychologically speaking, as those who primarily want to develop close relationships, become more self-aware, or contribute to the community. . . .
>
> People who value "extrinsic goals" like money, fame and beauty . . . are not only more depressed than others, but also report more behavioral problems and physical discomfort, as well as scoring lower on measures of vitality and self-actualization.[3]

No wonder those who scramble so hard after success keep asking themselves, "Is this all there is?" They are not getting closer to satisfaction and fulfillment in their headlong pursuit; they are actually vectoring in the opposite direction! But before you rush out to divest yourself of all signs of abundance, be aware that affluence in itself is not the problem. The article continues, "Affluence, per se, does not necessarily result in an unsatisfying life. Problems are primarily associated with 'living a life where that's your focus.'"[4]

As current research suggests, nothing is wrong with having plenty and acquiring more unless that's what you primarily live for. Aggressively seeking advancement and enjoying the accompanying perks and prestige are not negative pursuits unless you reserve time, effort, and interest for little else. That's the danger in the affluence-equals-success message; it can become all-consuming. Being infected by this inaccurate equation perpetrated by our culture can keep us from the very happiness we seek.

Authors John De Graaf, David Wann, and Thomas H. Naylor have coined a term for this condition. In their book, based on a PBS series, the authors state, "Amid the prosperity, the soaring economy and the superficial upbeat atmosphere marking the dawn of the new millennium, a powerful virus has infected American society, threatening our wallets, our friendships, our families, our communities, and our environment. We call the virus *Affluenza*."[5] Affluenza could best be described as a painful, contagious, socially transmitted condition of overload, debt, anxiety, and waste resulting from the dogged pursuit of more.

The book goes on to describe the harmful impact of Affluenza on our culture:

Affluenza's costs and consequences are immense, though often concealed. Untreated, the disease can cause permanent discontent. . . . In each of the past four years, more Americans declared personal bankruptcy than graduated from college. We have twice as many shopping centers as high schools. We now work more hours each year than do the citizens of any other industrial country, including Japan. Ninety-five percent of our workers say they wish they could spend more time with their families.[6]

As the magical snake oil elixirs in generations past, which purported to cure everything from warts to worry, achieving success through affluence is a myth. Clearly happiness, contentment, and fulfillment in life are found somewhere beyond accumulating money and things, power and prestige. What is the missing ingredient?

Choose Your Definition of Success

Imagine that you have received a phone call from Dr. Joe Bowen. His wife, Karen, has just served him with divorce papers. He wants you to meet him for coffee because he could use some company.

Sitting in the restaurant together, your conversation comes around to the topic of success. How do you think he might define success now? Can you hear him saying, "The money and the house and the snowmobiles are great, but real success is having a secure marriage and enjoying your work"?

You could probably sit down with Maggie Corelli, Gabe Dresser, and any number of success-driven, stressed-out individuals and hear the same kind of response. Even though our culture tends to equate success with achieving extrinsic goals, most people, when asked, will also define success in terms of intrinsic goals, such as:

36

- Success is coming home each day satisfied with my work.
- Success is having a warm relationship with my family.
- If I can learn to be content with my possessions, I will be successful.
- A life of integrity—that's what success is all about.
- I will feel like a success if I have a positive impact on other people.

Comments like these parallel what people have been saying for centuries about success, happiness, contentment, and fulfillment. For example:

- "Whoever does not regard what he has as most ample wealth is unhappy, though he is master of the world" (Epicurus).[7]
- "An aim in life is the only fortune worth finding" (Jacqueline Kennedy Onassis).[8]
- "Everything has its wonders, even darkness and silence, and I learn, whatever state I may be in, therein to be content" (Helen Keller).[9]
- "Our greatest happiness does not depend on the condition of life in which chance has placed us, but is always the result of a good conscience, good health, occupation and freedom in all just pursuits" (Thomas Jefferson).[10]
- "If any of you wants to be my follower, you must put aside your selfish ambition, shoulder your cross, and follow me. If you try to keep your life for yourself, you will lose it. But if you give up your life for me, you will find true life" (Jesus Christ).[11]

So your definition of success, and the way you live in pursuit of that definition, has everything to do with whether or not you experience a satisfying, fulfilling life. I believe that genuine success involves achieving both extrinsic *and* intrinsic goals. As the founder and CEO of a financial planning firm, I am committed to helping clients strategize, organize, and realize their maximum financial potential. But as a person whose core values encompass more than the financial/material world, I am even more deeply committed to helping people achieve what I call *true personal wealth.*

Dr. Joe Bowen is financially wealthy, but he is on the brink of bankruptcy in his marriage relationship and living at a poverty level when it comes to job satisfaction. In order to experience true personal wealth, Joe needs a vector change. He needs to give the same care and attention to nurturing his marriage and career that he already gives to his financial portfolio. He needs to pursue success in all areas simultaneously.

Maggie Corelli is experiencing abundance in her achievements but seriously lacking relational intimacy. As such, she is missing out on the satisfaction of true personal wealth, which embraces both. And our young friend Gabe Dresser is riding a rocket of success in his career, but that rocket could explode in his face if he does not broaden his definition of success to include enriching his relationships with his family and coworkers.

As a financial planner, I hope you are succeeding in your finances, and you may find some tips in the pages ahead that will be helpful. But this is not a book about financial planning. I have written this book for two specific reasons, which are broader than your financial portfolio.

First, I want to encourage you to begin measuring your success in terms of true personal wealth, which incorporates the whole of your life, not just the financial segment. Second, I want to coach you on how to implement the principles and practices of true personal wealth in your life through effective vector changes. It is my hope that you will find the chapters ahead infinitely more valuable than a book with a title like *Three Easy Steps to Becoming a Millionaire.*

A word of warning before we continue: Success in reaching many lofty extrinsic goals is relatively easy. For example, you can achieve financially simply by working hard while saving and investing wisely. We have all seen that formula work (and wish we had put it to work earlier in life ourselves). A young person starts putting a few dollars a week into a savings account and continues the habit over his working years, never taking anything out. By the time he is ready to retire, he is a millionaire. What could be easier?

You may also achieve a certain level of affluence incidentally by being in the right place at the right time, catching a few breaks, hitting a few hunches, and knowing the right people. You can marry the boss's kid—or the boss—inherit a half-million dollars from a long-lost uncle, pick the right lotto numbers, stumble onto a cure for cancer, or otherwise reach your goals for money, prestige, and power.

But if you choose to pursue true personal wealth, you won't stumble into it incidentally or by chance. You must be intentional and purposeful in your desire to achieve success across the board in your life. As in anything worthwhile, you must vector toward the target and keep doing so until you hit it. Benjamin Elijah Mays, mentor to the late Dr. Martin Luther King Jr., said, "The tragedy of life doesn't lie in not reaching your goal. The tragedy lies in having no goal to reach. It isn't a calamity to die with dreams unfulfilled, but it is a calamity not to dream. . . . It is not a disgrace not to reach the stars, but it is a disgrace to have no stars to reach for. Not failure but low aim is sin."[12]

The first step to achieving true personal wealth is to recognize how we become segmented in our pursuit of success. In the next chapter we will define personal integration and discuss why it is essential in our quest for true personal wealth.

Small Change *Challenges*

- Make a list of the "extrinsic" goals that you feel pressure to achieve in order to feel successful (e.g., retirement accounts, position, cars, house).
- Now make a list of the "intrinsic" goals you desire in life (e.g., happy marriage, good relationship with your children, good health).
- Circle the three most important items from each list, and write a two to three paragraph description of your personal success goals.

3

Are You Holding It All Together?

———————•———————

Not long ago I took an early morning flight from Des Moines to Chicago. Peering out the window as the plane descended into the Windy City during rush hour, I was struck by the sight below me. The city streets were gridlocked with cars inching bumper-to-bumper between streetlights in every direction. The freeways were anything but free as drivers jockeyed into position for the long crawl into the city. Elevated commuter trains rumbled toward the downtown district. I imagined those trains stuffed to the doors with dazed and dozing workers heading to their shops and offices.

Sure, we have rush hour in Des Moines, but not on this scale. And I've spent a lot of time in bustling big cities like Chicago, but this time the enormity of it all left me shaking my head. Tens of thousands of cars and hundreds of thousands of people all trying to get someplace at once, and they do it day after day. The same scene is played out in cities large and small across the country.

I thought about the hoard of people on the ground. Most of them were probably on their way to work. How many of them hated their jobs, despised their bosses, or were having extramarital affairs with their coworkers? How many would be promoted today? How many would be laid off or just quit? How many were stretched to the breaking point by demanding responsibilities? How many were hanging on by the fingernails until retirement?

Most of the people traveling across the city had left loved ones at home. How many of these commuters were struggling in dead or dying marriages? How many carried the pain of children who were involved in drugs, gangs, or other pitfalls? How many were estranged from parents or adult children? How many would return home today to a tormenting atmosphere of conflict, disrespect, hatred, or abuse?

On top of work and family responsibilities, these people doubtless carried other concerns and needs. Which ones were struggling with financial crises: more bills than money; evaporating retirement accounts; failing sales; critical business deals gone sour? How many of them had more things to do than hours to do them: school and carpool responsibilities with kids; church activities; civic responsibilities; parties and dates; club meetings; housework and gardening; fitness routines or sports activities? And if we were talking about your life, you could likely add in a few more items that tend to keep you on the run.

Landing at O'Hare that day, I mused about the millions of people across the country who feel trapped in a day in, day out journey on a treadmill they can't slow down or shut off. Their lives consist of a collection of mismatched pieces. They are vectoring in half a dozen directions at the same time. For these people, living is the frantic process of trying to hold it all together and make sense out of life.

It's Hard to Live When You're Struggling Just to Survive

That's the way it is for many of us, isn't it? We live in a culture driven by career and financial success; family, civic, and church responsibilities; and a jumbled assortment of other duties, deadlines, demands, and distractions. If the ideal life were compared to a leisurely swim across a beautiful lake, we'd seem to spend much of our time kicking and flailing just to keep from going under.

We might agree that life would be more sane and sensible if we got better organized. But who has time to slow down and do that? We yearn for a more balanced approach to schedule and responsibilities, but such yearnings are often steamrolled by the urgencies and emergencies of daily life. We might be more successful and satisfied in our endeavors if we prioritized them, but triage is a luxury we cannot afford.

Most people know intuitively there is more to life than just gritting it through the day-to-day. When I speak in seminars and conferences about true personal wealth, people nod their heads. We are convinced there is something better out there. We sense a higher calling to a truly successful and significant life. We long to soar above the rat race of making ends meet, getting the kids through college, surviving office politics, and so on. But daily life is so fractured and cluttered that we can't seem to get airborne. We are like those circus performers who spin cheap china plates atop long poles. We spend most of our energy just trying to prevent our many plates—family, career, finances, friendships—from crashing to the floor.

Furthermore, when we do find a quiet moment to consider such things as real success, purpose, and priorities in life, we don't know how to go about looking for them. And we get little help from the world around us. We are bombarded and befuddled by conflicting messages in the media, self-help books, advertising, self-styled "experts," religious leaders, and well-intentioned relatives and friends, all supposedly touting the "secret of success" or the "key to happiness." The pursuit of true personal wealth may be intriguing and inviting, but we can't seem to find the bridge to take us from where we are to where we want to be.

Personal Disintegration: Keeping the Plates Spinning

I call this mode of living the *disintegrating life syndrome.* Disintegration is the process of separating into parts, losing intactness, breaking up, deteriorating. This is an excellent description of so many today. People seem to be running six different directions at once—so much to do, so little time to do it. They frantically rush from wobbling plate to wobbling plate, trying to avert disaster. How can we get a handle on true personal wealth when our hands are so busy with plates?

Here's another word picture for the disintegrating life. Imagine the many areas of your life as an assortment of those plastic storage boxes we use in our cupboards or closets. Your marriage is in one box, and your life with your kids is in another. You have other boxes for your work, your friendships, your church activities, your finances, your recreation activities, and so on. Everything you're involved in is neatly compartmentalized.

The disintegrating individual moves from box to box as required, dealing with its demands and solving its problems. For example, things are running behind at work,

44

so you shove everything else to the back of the closet and dive into the box marked "Work" for the whole weekend. Or you are in charge of the annual fund-raiser for your club, so the rest of your life gets put on hold until the event is over. The dreaded "tyranny of the urgent" determines which area gets our attention next. And we keep shuffling the boxes around with little regard for how our actions in one area affect the others.

Sometimes we make a subtler decision to spend inappropriate amounts of time and energy in one box to the detriment or exclusion of others. For example, your near-addiction to sports keeps you glued to the TV every weekend, but your kids hardly see you. Or your fanatical involvement in your kids' activities turns your marriage into an emotional Sahara.

Notice that I'm talking about the *disintegrating* life— present tense—not the *disintegrated* life—past tense. Most people have not self-destructed—yet—but many are in the process of fragmenting their lives into separate and largely unrelated areas. The disintegrating life is a major roadblock to achieving true personal wealth.

Personal Integration: Learning to Juggle Life

It may sound simplistic, but the antidote to the *disintegrating* life is the *integrating* life. The two lifestyles are opposites. Where personal disintegration breaks the elements of our lives into separate, often unrelated parts, personal integration seeks to bring these many parts into a unified, harmonious, interrelated whole. Your responsibilities and challenges don't need to look like a collection of mismatched storage boxes stacked in a closet. You can integrate the many facets of your life into one manageable

45

"container" in which everything fits together and works together to help you achieve true personal wealth.

As you pursue an integrating life (not *integrated,* past tense, since this too is a process), you will begin to notice how each area affects all the others. For example, your personal proficiencies impact your success at work and any volunteering you do. The way you pursue your career affects the overall health of your relationships. The value you place on your family relates directly to your financial goals. In personal integration, no area of your life is an island unto itself. Your decisions and actions must be evaluated with a view to their ripple effect on your life as a whole, not just isolated parts of it.

Here is a quick, generalized overview of the contrast between these two opposing approaches to life. Which list more closely typifies your life today?

The Disintegrating Life	The Integrating Life
Focuses on the pieces	Focuses on the whole
Tends to compartmentalize	Tends to unify
Evaluates based on urgency	Evaluates based on priority
Lives reactively	Lives proactively
Driven by wants and desires	Driven by needs and values
More concerned with quantity	More concerned with quality
Largely random and unbalanced	Largely ordered and balanced
Leads to complacency or burnout	Leads to peace and satisfaction

Here's a more visual way to view the contrast. As described earlier, the disintegrating life is like running from pole to pole keeping a number of plates spinning. But the integrating life is like juggling a number of balls simultaneously. Now, these two images may seem similar to you, the goal being to keep the many areas of your life from crashing to the floor. But plate spinning and ball juggling are very different. Let's take a closer look at the skill of juggling and see why its principles are so

46

appropriate and necessary to achieving true personal wealth.

In their insightful article, "Juggling Life," Thomas Addington and Stephen Graves compare the dexterity of juggling balls, bowling pins, and knives to the skill of being what they term a *life juggler*. Michael Moschen, one of the world's greatest jugglers, has said, "Anyone can learn to juggle. . . . It's about breaking down complex patterns and maneuvers into simple tasks. Juggling is a system of tosses and throws, of different patterns that, once broken down, understood and mastered, can be put together to create something magical."[1] He was talking about life as well as a handful of balls.

A vital element of both juggling and the integrating life is balance. You might assume that perfect balance means stillness, having everything under control. But in juggling balls and life, balance does not mean holding everything still. Juggler Moschen comments, "[Balance is] the ability to make exquisitely refined responses to any unexpected change. It's the sense of little movements creating perfect-yet-temporary equilibrium."[2] That's not exactly how we would describe the art of plate spinning, is it?

Addington and Graves provide us with an application of a juggler's balance to the integrating life. They write, "Balance is the ability to continually recognize and juggle the multidimensional assignments and opportunities of life."[3] You have likely used the phrase "I have too many balls in the air" to describe a particularly stressful day, week, or life. It means we're having difficulty keeping up with our many responsibilities, relationships, and problems. Some of them are falling through the cracks.

We all have that problem occasionally—sometimes more than occasionally. But, as Moschen reminds us, the balance of juggling is a learned skill, with a handful of balls or with a life full of experiences and responsibilities. Pursuing true personal wealth through a life of integration requires that we submit to the discipline of learning balance. Addington and Graves have a few helpful insights.

Balance is not static; it changes because our circumstances continually change. The fluctuating needs of your kids as they grow older; the changing dynamics of your work as you advance through your career; the variables that affect your stock portfolio as the market rises and falls; plus all the unexpected glitches, gaffes, crises, and tragedies that attend life mean we must continually adjust to maintain good balance.

A life of balance begins with the awareness of the many facets of our lives and the impact they have on us. Since we all have blind spots, we must seek the wisdom and counsel of others who can help us see where our lives may be out of balance at any given time. Therefore we are wise to schedule regular times of quiet evaluation and assessment with those who know us best: spouse, boss, trusted friend, minister, financial advisor.

Balance requires juggling all the balls simultaneously. "The death knell in juggling is to watch any individual object," juggler Moschen says. "Our instinct is to look at each ball or task separately, because we want to have control." That's the life of the plate spinner—focusing on one plate at a time while the others lose momentum. Successful life juggling is the ability to keep multiple tasks in the air while recognizing that the one we have in our hand—for whatever length of time—is the one we need to concentrate on. A primary skill of balance is focusing on one thing at a time while performing multiple tasks.

Balance in our multidimensional lives means decisions, decisions, decisions. We are all multidimensional. Each of us deals every day with issues related to family, work, finances, community, faith, and so on. Sometimes two or more dimensions demand our attention at the same time. We have to juggle all the aspects of life all the time, requiring us to make choices, sometimes painful ones. For example, does a father accompany his nervous child to his first sports camp, or does he attend an important strategic planning session at work? Does a manager work late so she can make sure the project due tomorrow is as good as it can be, or does she go to her monthly small group leaders meeting at church?

Taken individually, decisions like these don't seem too overwhelming. But if we continually choose work over family, or community over self, or leisure over responsibility, at some point all the balls will hit the floor at once.[4]

A life of personal integration doesn't mean you won't drop the ball—or *balls*—from time to time. You are imperfect, and you live in an imperfect world. But as you learn to juggle and hone your balance through the process of integrating all your experiences, you will steadily increase your net worth of true personal wealth.

A Vision for True Personal Wealth

In light of this contrast between integration and disintegration, what might be a picture of true personal wealth for you? Try this exercise.

Imagine living with a clear picture of how all the parts of your life fit together.

Imagine realizing a healthy perspective of the many demands on your life and grasping a plan for dealing with them in a cohesive and productive manner.

Imagine gaining a firm grip on your purpose in life—why you are here—allowing you to crystallize your life goals, integrate and balance your many responsibilities and opportunities, and prioritize your daily activities.

Imagine the satisfaction and fulfillment of knowing that you are vectoring toward success by amassing wealth, not only financially and materially but relationally, intellectually, emotionally, spiritually, and experientially.

Take some time in the next day or week to evaluate these areas of your life. To what extent are they in balance or out of balance? The rest of this book will give you options for achieving a healthy balance in all areas of life.

Finally, imagine the prospect of "bequeathing" your multifaceted wealth—not just your estate but your experiences, wisdom, and influence—to your children, grandchildren, and others within your sphere of relationships.

Can you see yourself in this new paradigm for wealth? Do you have a sense of how rewarding and satisfying it can be? This vision for true personal wealth in your life can become a reality. This book will help you begin to implement that vision for today and prepare a legacy that will outlive you for generations.

Small Change *Challenges*

- Think about all of the important areas of your life— marriage, children, work, friendships, spiritual, financial, physical fitness, health, and so forth. Would you describe your life as integrating or disintegrating?
- What is one small lifestyle change that could positively impact at least three of those areas?

Part 2

The Path to True Personal Wealth

4

A Life Rich with Experiences

How do you think a typical person in the mall would complete this statement: "Wealthy is the person who . . ."? No matter where you live in the United States and how many people you talk to, you would likely get a number of different responses to that statement, including several of the following:

- Wealthy is the person who has a billion dollars.
- Wealthy is the person who enjoys good health.
- Wealthy is the person who has a loving, supportive spouse and children.
- Wealthy is the person who can pay all the bills each month.
- Wealthy is the person who has achieved his or her life goals.

The Path to True Personal Wealth

- Wealthy is the person who has a satisfying career.
- Wealthy is the person who is respected by his or her peers.
- Wealthy is the person who is at peace with God.
- Wealthy is the person who can retire comfortably.

When I ask people in my seminars, "What is your definition of wealth?" their responses tend toward financial and material values. But when I ask them to complete the statement "Wealthy is the person who . . . ," most people are more contemplative and altruistic in their answers. Recently I spoke to a group of more than a hundred realtors and asked them to complete that statement. Not one of their responses was financial; all had to do with relational, emotional, or spiritual values.

Wealth is a relative term. To the person who lives hand-to-mouth, wealth has a lot to do with money. But, as we saw with Dr. Joe Bowen, some people who are rolling in money would gladly trade it all for a happy marriage or satisfaction in their work or a clear conscience. So the definitions of wealth are virtually limitless, unique to every individual. When you begin to realize how multidimensional wealth is, you are in a position to discover the nature of true personal wealth.

The Nature of True Personal Wealth

The term I have coined for true personal wealth is life-Wealth. I define it this way:

lifeWealth: *The accumulation of financial, relational, physical, intellectual, and spiritual capital.*

54

LifeFocus means bringing into balance the five dimensions of wealth accessible to every one of us. Let me define them for you.

1. Financial capital. This is perhaps the most obvious and easily measured dimension. It includes your money, assets, and material possessions—what a financial planner might identify as your "total net worth."

2. Relational capital. This dimension refers to all the people in your life: spouse, children, parents, siblings, extended family, friends, coworkers, neighbors, and acquaintances.

3. Physical capital. Here we're talking about your physical well-being: health, wellness, fitness, and recreation.

4. Intellectual capital. Under this umbrella you can put your personal proficiencies: IQ and aptitudes plus formal education, self-directed learning, job training, skill development, and unique abilities.

5. Spiritual capital. This dimension encompasses the place God and faith occupy in your life.

Remember: We must view our lives as an integrated whole, not a collection of separate, unrelated parts. These five dimensions are not like separate plates we frantically keep spinning but rather like a collection of balls we learn to juggle and balance simultaneously.

These five lifeWealth dimensions are categories of life experience. The term "life experience" covers everything we do, everything that happens to us in the course of day-to-day life, good and bad. Our many and varied experiences in life are the means by which we accumulate and manage lifeWealth. With every experience we have the opportunity to increase our overall lifeWealth.

Take the area of financial capital, for example. Most of us *accumulate* a significant portion of our financial capital through work experiences. There are other financial "experiences," of course, such as receiving gifts or an inheritance, winning the lottery, selling goods or property. But most everyone knows experientially what it means to receive salary or wages in exchange for some kind of labor or service. And many of us understand the sad experiences of downsizing, layoffs, and unemployment, which negatively affect the accumulation of financial capital.

We *manage* financial capital through our personal, day-to-day experiences with the money we have. Sometimes we manage our money well through profitable experiences: careful spending, prudent saving, and wise investing. At other times we manage it poorly through lack of planning, bad decisions, carelessness, and wastefulness. These experiences with money and material possessions determine the bottom line of our financial capital.

Let me further illustrate using the dimension of relational capital. We all "inherited" relational capital—relationships with people—at birth: parents, siblings, and extended family. We continue to *accumulate* relational capital as we gain friends, marry, produce children, and participate in a variety of social experiences. We *manage* our relational capital by how we treat and are treated by the people in our lives. These ongoing relational experiences directly impact the bottom line of our relational capital.

The same is true across all dimensions of life. Physical capital generally increases with proper diet, exercise, recreation, and rest and decreases when we ignore these guidelines. Intellectual capital increases as we make the most of our unique abilities, expand our knowledge through reading, and continue to sharpen our work skills and decreases when we refuse to develop in these ways. And spiritual capital grows as we actively seek to develop a relationship with God through Bible study, prayer, faith, and obedience and diminishes when we usurp God's role in our lives.

56

These key dimensions of wealth are to be fully integrated. Our lifeFocus grows sharper as we accumulate and profitably manage life experiences as a whole, not in one or two isolated dimensions. Developing your financial and intellectual capital while ignoring your relational capital reduces your net wealth. Focus on your physical capital without also accumulating spiritual capital and you are poorer for it.

I can further illustrate this principle by using another word picture relating to the world of finance.

Banking Your Experiences

You no doubt keep track of your financial capital through an assortment of accounts at your bank: checking, savings, interest-bearing, money market, and so on. You may also have a collection of investments: stocks and bonds, mutual funds, annuities, IRAs. Everything having to do with your money—where it is, how it's allocated, how much it's earning in interest and dividends—is your *financial portfolio*.

You don't need a money expert to grasp the basics of managing a financial portfolio. Your deposits in and credits to that portfolio contribute to your overall equity. Your withdrawals from and debits to those accounts contribute to your debt. As long as you deposit more than you withdraw, you build up equity and grow in wealth. And the larger your financial portfolio grows, the more money you have to meet your needs and wants for the future. But when withdrawals consistently exceed your deposits, you move in the direction of debt and eventual bankruptcy.

Similarly, we all have what I like to call an *experience portfolio*. Your experience portfolio is like an invisible bank account in which your many life experiences, and your responses to them, are tallied. Every experience has great value. I'm not talking about monetary value, of course; your life experiences are worth much more than mere money, although people sometimes don't view them that way. Your experience portfolio increases as you accumulate and profitably manage your life experiences.

By life experiences, I mean two things. First, experiences include everything *you do,* from the mundane to the ordinary to the exciting, from once-in-a-lifetime happenings to everyday routines. Second, they include everything that happens *to you,* pleasure and pain, triumph and tragedy. For example, any given day can include a wide range of experiences: a pleasant conversation with your spouse, an argument with your child, an encounter with a homeless person on the street, lunch with a friend, closing—or failing to close—an important deal at work, a fender bender on the way home, the sudden death of a loved one, a deeply moving program on TV. Life itself is one experience after another, and for most of us, these experiences overlap to the point that we really do feel as if we're juggling several balls at the same time.

As with your finances, you have a choice as to what you will do with your experiences. You can "bank" them in your experience portfolio or you can squander them. The experiences you bank are like deposits in or credits to your experience portfolio, building your lifeWealth. How do you "deposit" an experience? Like depositing money in your bank account, in effect you tuck each experience away in a safe place for future use. It's the disciplined exercise of taking something positive from everything that happens in your life. Here are a few examples:

- Playing backyard soccer with your kids, you realize that you're a little out of shape. You determine to dust off the old treadmill in the basement and start building up your stamina. Your decision adds to your physical capital, increasing your overall lifeWealth.

- Your company encourages you to pursue a master's degree, promising a substantial raise when you do. It will cost you some money and a couple evenings a week for class and study time, but you decide to do it. The experience will net you additional intellectual and financial capital.

- You have a heated argument with your spouse. The conflict is your fault, but you don't want to admit it. If you don't back down, things will just get worse. So you swallow your pride and apologize. Your action is a deposit of relational capital, increasing the bottom line in your experience portfolio.

- Attending the funeral of a relative, you can't help but contemplate the age-old questions: Why am I here? Where am I going when I die? *It wouldn't hurt to get back to church and find some answers,* you reason. You are on the verge of banking some spiritual capital, enriching your experience portfolio.

In each of your experiences, as in the examples above, you can choose to squander the opportunity instead of banking it. You can blow off your exercise program, the master's degree, your apology to your spouse, a spiritual quest, and so on. Every day brings life experiences we fail to manage profitably for whatever reason. Whenever we ignore an opportunity to learn or grow from a life experience, it's like tossing money into the fire. We are turning potential profit into loss.

Here are three additional key thoughts about your experience portfolio.

1. All experiences, good and bad, can be a deposit in your experience portfolio. As you know, life is made up of good and bad experiences. Sometimes we do things right, and sometimes we foul them up. Today you feel like a million bucks, but tomorrow the flu may knock you flat. The bear and the bull fight over your money daily in the stock market, and sometimes the bear wins. Your spouse was warm and cuddly last night but may be cold and prickly tonight. On some days everything goes your way, and on other days you can't win no matter how you try. But most days we get a little bit of both. That's just the way life is. As the wise writer of Ecclesiastes once wrote, "When times are good, be happy; but when times are bad, consider: God has made the one as well as the other."[1]

Whether an experience is good or bad does not determine if you can profit from it; what you do with that experience makes it "bankable." For example, let's say your stock portfolio takes a big dive. You can kick the dog out of frustration or put your fist through a wall in anger. Will it do you any good? Probably not, and you may have to deal with a snarling dog or a broken hand. But if you learn from that experience by talking to your broker and adjusting your portfolio, your bad day at the market may lead to many good days of investing. That's taking your bad experience "to the bank."

Similarly, an argument with your teenage child can result in three days of cold silence between you or a heart-to-heart chat that brings greater understanding and intimacy. Being laid off from work can send you into depression or help you find the doorway to a new career better suited to your abilities and temperament. A debilitating injury can leave you feeling robbed of your strength or spur you on to develop new strengths. Every bad experience comes to us with the potential of a good outcome that, if acted upon, will accrue in our experience portfolio as a deposit.

A captivating and inspiring story is told in the Bible about a man named Joseph.[2] As a Hebrew youth, Joseph was despised by his ten older brothers, who sold him into slavery in Egypt, explaining to their father that he had been killed by a wild beast. Joseph, a godly man, worked hard and became chief servant in the household of an Egyptian official. The commander's wife tried to seduce Joseph. When he refused, she accused him of sexual assault, landing Joseph in prison.

Yet Joseph's faith in God did not waver, and eventually his ability to interpret dreams and prepare Egypt for widespread famine catapulted him to second in command to the pharaoh himself. The famine brought Joseph's brothers to Egypt to buy food from the ruler. They had no idea he was their long-lost brother. When Joseph finally revealed himself to them, they feared for their lives because of what they had done to him. Joseph's response helps us see how to respond to our bad experiences. He told his brothers: "You intended to harm me, but God intended it for good to accomplish what is now being done, the saving of many lives."[3]

Some people seem to spend their lives avoiding bad experiences—problems, pain, struggle, loss, trouble, sorrow, failure. And when they do have a bad experience, they either wallow in self-pity or run away in denial, brushing it off as nothing. Now, I'm not saying that you should live carelessly or go looking for trouble. Just be realistic and opportunistic. Bad things happen, even to good people. When you learn to look for the good in your bad experiences, you will have twice as much capital to deposit in your experience portfolio.

Often an experience and its immediate outcome are not what benefit your experience portfolio. Some experiences are so horrible that you will be hard-pressed to find any redeeming value in them. Especially in these situations, the valuable deposits come in the form of the wisdom, knowledge, or insight you gain from the experience. You will be able to bank what you learn from those experiences, how they prepare you for facing other situations in life, and how they equip you for helping others facing similar situations.

When I entered the eighth grade, I was all pumped up to play football. Like every school athlete, I had to be cleared by a doctor in order to play. The routine physical exam resulted in a big shock to my parents and me. The doctor informed us that I had a heart ailment requiring surgery. To make matters worse, during the surgery the doctors found a spot on my lung that they suspected might be cancerous. So instead of being released after heart surgery, I was detained in the hospital for possible exploratory surgery on my lung. I was scared because kids my age just didn't have heart problems or cancer. I also felt alone because the hospital was two hours from my home and I didn't have many visitors.

At one point I was feeling pretty low. Being away from home, I was lonely and felt sorry for myself. As I wandered the halls of the hospital, one day I found myself in the burn unit. Peering into room after room of patients suffering from severe burns, I thought, *I really don't have it so bad.* From that point on, whenever I felt fearful or sorry for myself, I took another walk through the burn unit. I always returned to my room with a different attitude. The cancer tests came back negative, so I was finally released.

My wife says that I am an eternal optimist, and I suppose I am. I believe my positive outlook on negative circumstances may have begun when I was a scared thirteen-year-old in the halls of that hospital. Heart surgery and the fear of cancer had no redeeming value for me—other than repairing my heart. But what I learned about bad circumstances and how to respond to them has been invaluable in shaping my optimistic outlook.

2. *Your response to your bad experiences determines whether or not they will credit or debit your experience portfolio.* The following story captures well the importance of a positive outlook on unpleasant experiences.

The 92-year-old, petite, well-poised and proud mother-in-law of my best friend, who is fully dressed each morning by eight o'clock, with her hair fashionably coifed and makeup perfectly applied, even though she is legally blind, moved to a nursing home today. Her husband of 70 years recently passed away, making the move necessary. Maurine Jones is the most lovely, gracious, dignified woman that I have ever had the pleasure of meeting. While I have never aspired to attain her depth of wisdom, I do pray that I will learn from her vast experience. After many hours of waiting patiently in the lobby of the nursing home, she smiled sweetly when told her room was ready.

As she maneuvered her walker to the elevator, I provided a visual description of her tiny room, including the eyelet sheets that had been hung on her window. "I love it," she stated with the enthusiasm of an eight-year-old having just been presented with a new puppy. "Mrs. Jones, you haven't seen the room . . . just wait."

"That doesn't have anything to do with it," she replied. "Happiness is something you decide on ahead of time. Whether I like my room or not doesn't depend on how the furniture is arranged . . . it's how I arrange my mind. I already decided to love it . . .

"It's a decision I make every morning when I wake up. I have a choice; I can spend the day in bed recounting the difficulty I have with the parts of my body that no longer work, or get out of bed and be thankful for the ones that do. Each day is a gift, and as long as my eyes open, I'll focus on the new day and all the happy memories I've stored away

63

. . . just for this time in my life. Old age is like a bank account . . . you withdraw from what you've put in. So, my advice to you would be to deposit a lot of happiness in the bank account of memories."[4]

As this sweet old lady discovered, you can bank your bad experiences as assets when you decide ahead of time to make the best of them. It's all in how you "arrange your mind."

3. *Regular deposits in your experience portfolio build up a reserve from which you can draw in the future.* Mrs. Jones had the right idea. She had saved up more than enough happiness over the decades to get her through the difficulties of old age. Just as you deposit money in your bank account for future expenses, financial emergencies, and retirement, your consistent deposits of life experiences—good and bad—accrue in your experience portfolio for your future use.

In contrast, those who respond negatively to their experiences—particularly the bad ones—are heading toward experiential bankruptcy. They are destined to make the same mistakes repeatedly and have little or nothing to draw from or share with others. Their lives are marked by frustration, dissatisfaction, unhappiness, lack of fulfillment, and poverty.

You may be asking, "What can I possibly withdraw from an account filled with past experiences?" I can think of several things: knowledge and wisdom gained from trial and error; patience; contentment. For example, having worked through relationship conflicts in the past, you draw from your experience portfolio to resolve present conflicts more effectively. Having applied yourself to excel in your business, you go to your experience portfolio to assist others in solving work-related problems. Having dealt with the numerous challenges of child raising, you find in your experience portfolio proven advice to share with younger parents.

You have a choice about what you do with your money. You can spend it as fast or faster than you earn it and face a retirement of poverty, living off your relatives, living off the state, or living on the street. Or you can manage your funds wisely, building up a nest egg for retirement and an inheritance for your children. It's a no-brainer, isn't it? Who in their right mind would consciously choose to live so irresponsibly? It reminds me of the old proverb: "Of what use is money in the hand of a fool, since he has no desire to get wisdom?"[5]

You have essentially the same choice with your life experiences, which are the currency of true personal wealth. The more experiences you bank, the greater your reserve for future enjoyment and to share with others. Who in their right mind would want to squander such wealth?

There is great value in banking our *past* experiences as well as *present* experiences. I call this process "recapturing equity" in your experience portfolio. You recapture equity by periodically reviewing your personal history and past experiences, good and bad, in order to glean good from them. Here's a way this can be done.

Sit down with a sheet of paper and begin listing past experiences. Many people struggle at first to recall some of their experiences. However, over time they will flood back to your memory. One way to encourage the process is to focus on one small period of your life at a time, such as childhood, teenage years, college experiences, or early marriage. As memories come to mind, start writing and don't stop until you can't think of any more.

Once you have a sheet full of history and experiences, read through your list and identify those that are most significant. Make a separate list of these. Contemplate each experience thoroughly, trying to recapture the wisdom, knowledge, and insight you gained—or may now gain—from it. How has that experience contributed positively to who you are today? How has it positioned you to be helpful to others? How has it equipped you for future experiences and decisions? As you think about each experience in this way, you will begin to think about it more positively, helping you recapture equity from that experience.

Create Your Future Today

Not only can you recapture equity from the past, you can also begin the process of building future equity in your experience portfolio. In order to do this, you need to envision your positive future. We call this a "life reflection exercise." Here is an example:

Imagine this scenario: See yourself in your nineties, something like old Mrs. Jones in the story above, moving a little slowly but still mentally sharp. You step out onto the deck of your cabin by the lake, a favorite vacation spot of yours for decades. You ease into a comfortable chair to enjoy another glorious sunset. Caught up in the wonder of the moment, you begin to reflect on your long and pleasant life. The memories flood back, and even the stunning radiance of the setting sun is no match for the glow of satisfaction and fulfillment that warms your heart.

Putting yourself in this ideal setting, what do you hope you could say about the life you have experienced? In other words, what would you like to see on the bottom line of your experience portfolio as your life draws to a close? Don't be timid; aim high. Here are several descriptive sentences to help you formulate your own picture of true personal wealth.

Financial capital. I met all my financial obligations responsibly. I enjoyed my material possessions. I was generous toward others in need and held enough in reserve for a comfortable retirement. I planned for and eliminated the fear of the unexpected in my finances.

Relational capital. I cherish the deep love of family members. I am enriched by many close friendships. I have enjoyed the respect of coworkers and been a positive influence in the life of everyone I met. I have no unresolved conflicts or issues in my key relationships.

Physical capital. I stayed on top of personal health and fitness. I struck a reasonable balance between work and recreation and have enjoyed relatively good health.

Intellectual capital. I made the most of my natural skills and abilities. I worked hard and well in the areas of my responsibility, and my conscientious efforts resulted in significant contributions to my world. I was a "lifetime learner," always stretching myself to know more and perform better.

Spiritual capital. I am at peace with my Creator. I have discovered and lived out his purpose for my life and am ready to meet him when I die.

Now here's the big question: If you want to summarize your life in glowing terms such as these—and who wouldn't?—how are you vectoring toward that outcome today? You won't be able to enjoy a carefree retirement in twenty or thirty years if you're not building your financial portfolio today. In a similar way, if you want to conclude your life with a healthy experience portfolio as suggested in the statements above, you need to be making regular deposits in those accounts today.

You may lament, "I'll never be able to make those statements. My life is half over and I've spent most of it on myself. Looking at my experience portfolio today, I'm nearly broke."

Don't despair. As someone has said, there are two best times to plant an oak tree. The first best time was twenty years ago; the next best time is today. Everyone has regrets about missed opportunities. For example, how many investors wish they had bought into an obscure little acorn back in the 1980s called Microsoft, which has grown into a mighty financial oak? How many of us wish we had spent more time with our kids when they were younger, stayed in better physical condition, taken the dream job instead of the best-paying job, or retained our childlike trust in God?

You can't change your past, but you can change your future. You can plant an oak today by committing to and taking steps toward acquiring true personal wealth. In the chapters ahead, I will show you how.

Small Change *Challenges*

- Take a few minutes and write down your thoughts regarding the "Life Reflection" exercise.
- Decide on three action steps you could take in the next thirty days that could move you closer to your desired life outcome. Write them down and share them with your spouse or a close friend.

5

An Overview of Your Life

———————————•———————————

Life comes to each of us in three distinct phases. Understanding these stages will help you grasp how each experience and circumstance contributes to who you are, what you have to offer, and what you will become.

Phase One—Foundation
Birth to Midtwenties

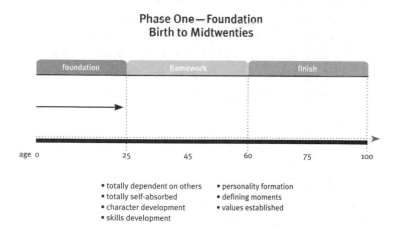

You came into this world totally dependent on others to meet your vital needs. The adults in your life, principally your parents, did for you what you could not do for yourself. And in those early years, you occupied the center of your universe. Everything revolved around you. If you didn't get what you wanted—a meal, a clean diaper, a toy, attention—somebody heard about it through your loud protests.

During the childhood years of this phase, a number of foundation stones were laid. Your personality took shape. You probably inherited some traits genetically, but your personality was also formed through parental influence.

My wife, Nancy, and I intentionally contributed to our kids' personalities when they were young. A couple of them were shy by nature, but we didn't want them to be hermits or wallflowers when it came to social interaction. We believe that everybody needs to know how to meet people and demonstrate genuine interest. So we instituted the "five question rule" in our family. Whenever we were invited to a social gathering such as a wedding, a party, or an open house, our kids had instructions to engage the people they met by asking at least five conversation-starting questions. We helped them come up with their questions ahead of time, such as, "How do you know the bride and groom?" "How long have you lived in the community?" "Where do you go to school?" They had to ask their questions and report back to us later.

Our kids didn't like this rule. But today, as young adults, their personalities are more outgoing than they would have been otherwise, and they are confident in most social situations.

Your personality is a combination of your genetic makeup, the training you received from your elders, and even some negative influences, such as an abusive or smothering parent. For better or for worse, much of your personality was shaped during the first several years of your life.

Many of your attitudes were also formed during the childhood years. I am an early riser today—bounding out of bed at daybreak ready to charge into the day—because of my father's influence. When I was a boy, Dad woke up my brothers and me every morning by coming into our rooms whistling reveille. We hated that piercing sound, but no matter how loudly we complained, Dad kept whistling until our feet hit the floor. I think Dad's whistling changed my attitude about the importance of getting up and getting going in the morning.

Much of your character and value system was also shaped during the early years of this foundation phase. Like your personality, these traits were largely impressed upon you by your parents and other significant adults in your life. For example, I can trace the long-standing value of honesty and truthfulness in my life to an incident that happened when I was eleven. I had walked down to the neighborhood store and stolen a candy bar. When I got home, my father caught me with the candy and asked where I got it. I was busted and had to confess. Dad made me walk back to the store—while he followed me all the way in the car—and apologize to the store owner. I was mortified. That incident changed my life, and I have never stolen anything since.

Many of your skills were also developed during the foundation phase. If you grew up in an athletic family, you probably learned to throw, catch, run, and shoot baskets. If your parents had musical abilities, you likely learned to sing or play an instrument. Depending on what your parents and older siblings enjoyed, you may have acquired skills for sewing, cooking, woodworking, gardening, decorating, and so on.

71

You continued to acquire skills as a youth when you entered the workforce. Every job you had as a kid—whether delivering newspapers, baby-sitting, flipping burgers, picking fruit, or waiting tables—equipped you with new skills. You may have acquired a trade by working in your family's business. It's possible that you make your living today using skills you acquired as a child or youth.

The foundation phase is also where you developed your concept of God. If you attended Sunday school, church services, mass, or synagogue as a child, your first thoughts of God were likely formulated from what you heard and saw. And if your family had no religious affiliation, your theological views were influenced by what your parents communicated about God and faith, both verbally and through their actions.

As you matured, your concept of God may have changed due to the influence of your peers. Kids who come out of childhood with strong religious convictions are sometimes lured away from faith during their teen years by a secular crowd. Conversely, some kids with no religious background find faith in God through the influence of a youth ministry of some kind.

Opening Your Experience Account

In many families, when a baby is born the parents or grandparents open a bank account in the child's name and begin making regular deposits. The account may be designated for college education, wedding costs, a car, or whatever. The child is oblivious to this nest egg for years. It's his account, but he had nothing to do with what's in it.

Even if your family did not provide a bank account for you, they did open another account for you when you were born—your experience account. You began accumulating

72

life experiences from day one. However, most of the "deposits" during your childhood were made by parents, older siblings, or other significant adults in your life. In other words, day-to-day life was the product of what others did to you, with you, and for you. You were too young to direct your own affairs. Somebody else decided where you would live, what you would eat, what you would wear, when you would sleep, and how you would be treated. And all these experiences were stashed away in your experience portfolio. Long before you even knew what was happening, you were drawing on experiences that others had deposited in your life.

By and large, experiences during our early years of development were positive. Most parents love their children and seek to do what's best for them. So you likely grew up in a healthy, caring environment, stocking your experience portfolio with many rich deposits.

But parents are only human. They make mistakes. They are not always loving and caring. So some of our childhood experiences were less than pleasant. You may have been punished too harshly at times. You may have been neglected, abandoned, or abused in some way by a parent. These things happened *to* you; they weren't your fault. Though these experiences also ended up in your experience portfolio, they did not contribute to your true personal wealth. They were a debit rather than a credit, as if someone made a withdrawal from your bank account without your permission.

Everyone suffered some negative experiences as innocent children. Depending on the frequency and severity of your experiences, you may have arrived at adulthood with a very low balance in your experience portfolio, more debt than equity, bordering on bankruptcy. There was little or nothing you could do about it then, but you can do something about it now, as I will explain later in this chapter.

From Dependence to Independence

Growing through infancy, childhood, and adolescence to young adulthood, we transition from utter dependence on parents and others to increasing levels of independence. As such, more of our life experiences are the product of our own activities, choices, and relationships. In other words, we start making our own deposits to—and withdrawals from—our experience portfolio even as parents and others continue to influence our lives.

But since we are no closer to being perfect than our parents were, we also cause some costly debits to our experience portfolio. You can likely recall your share of foolish mistakes, irresponsible choices, and bullheaded rebellion as a teen or young adult that ended up costing you personally. Maybe you gambled away some money; alienated a parent, sibling, or friend; got fired from a job or two because of laziness; or killed off a few million brain cells experimenting with drugs.

"If I had it to do over again," we all say, "I would have done some things differently." But since we can't undo everything harmful we have done, we have to deal with the shortfall in our accounts. At the least, some of these unpleasant experiences may have deterred us from other bad choices later in life.

The Impact of Defining Events

The foundation phase can be significantly enhanced or scarred by one or more "defining events." These are momentous, extraordinary experiences that change the course of our lives in some way. On the negative side, a defining moment for a child may be the death of a parent or sibling, the separation or divorce of parents, family bankruptcy, the arrest of a parent, or rape or sexual abuse by a trusted relative. World-rocking events like these can seriously deplete your experience portfolio, sometimes requiring years of positive inflow to heal the damage.

There are also defining events that positively impact the experience portfolio, such as a windfall that pulls a family out of poverty and into financial security, the miraculous healing of a life-threatening disease, the restoration of a broken family, or a life-changing spiritual experience. Defining events like these in your life can serve as a major deposit in your experience portfolio, providing a deep reserve as you move through the next two phases of life.

Phase Two — Framework
Early Twenties to Early Sixties

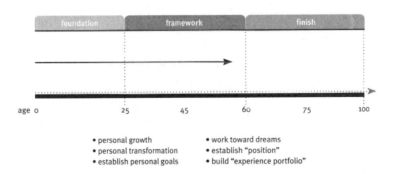

During the framework phase, we build our lives on the foundation that was laid during the first twenty-plus years. This phase is launched by a personal transformation that occurs at some point in early adulthood: the realization that we are now responsible for what we do and what we

75

become. Parents and teachers no longer direct our activities or control our behavior. We are full-fledged adults, free to make our own choices: how to spend money, whom to have as friends, whom to marry, where to live, how to make a living, whose influence to accept, what to believe about God, and so on.

Much of your education in the foundation phase was programmed into you. You were forced to attend school up to a certain age. Even your college education may have been more your parents' idea than yours as they paid for and pressured you to earn a degree. But in the framework stage, you don't have to take another hour of classes if you don't want to. The onus for your continuing education and whom you will look to for influence and guidance now rests squarely on your shoulders. This is the time to let go of any tendencies to maintain a "victim's mentality." We can't hang on to the past. We must take control of our own capacity to live life and make our own deposits. No more excuses; the buck stops here.

I remember when the reality of responsibility really hit me. Nancy and I were newly married, but I was still an irresponsible young buck in a lot of ways. I had pawned off managing the family finances onto Nancy. My idea of balancing a checkbook was to change banks.

I'll never forget the day Nancy threw the checkbook at me and snapped, "All right, you're in charge now." What a wake-up call! My wife had tossed our finances into my lap—literally. She wasn't going to do it, and my parents certainly weren't going to do it, so I had to step up to the plate and take responsibility. It was a major turning point in my life.

Our son Ryan had a similar transformation.

Not too long ago, Ryan got married. One day I received a phone call from him. "Hey, Dad, I have a question about

76

our insurance." He also had numerous questions and concerns about saving and spending. Ryan thanked me and hung up. In the following weeks he called a few more times with financial questions. During one of our conversations, Ryan said, "You know, Dad, this is kind of fun." I had to smile.

Ryan had come face-to-face with the reality that he was now responsible for the finances of his new household. It was a personal transformation that catapulted him into the framework phase of his life.

Managing Your Life Experience Portfolio

The transition from foundation to framework means that you assume responsibility for your life experiences in all the dimensions of wealth—financial capital, relational capital, physical capital, intellectual capital, and spiritual capital. Only you can initiate action in these areas if you are to experience true personal wealth. Mom, Dad, and others may still try to tell you what to do, and their counsel and advice can still be of value. But you alone are responsible for the bottom line in the five accounts of your experience portfolio.

The buck stops with you in dealing with life experiences *proactively* by answering such questions as:

Financial Capital
How much life insurance will you carry on yourself? Your spouse?
Does your employer have a retirement plan? How will you supplement that plan?
Who will write the checks month by month: You? Your spouse? The two of you together?

What limits will you set for credit card debt?

Will you implement a strategy for charitable and church giving?

Relational Capital

Where will you spend Thanksgiving and Christmas— with your family or your spouse's family?

Which friends will you trust to give you good advice?

What are you willing to do to keep your marriage relationship positive and healthy?

How much time will you invest in your kids' extracurricular activities?

Physical Capital

What will you do to keep yourself physically fit?

How will you balance work with recreation?

Will you schedule periodic routine checkups with physicians, dentist, and so on?

How much sleep do you need every night?

Intellectual Capital

Is your job best suited to your skills and training?

What is your work goal: best-paying job or most fulfilling job?

Are you a company person or do you want to work for yourself?

What will you do to continue your personal growth?

How will you use your skills and abilities outside your job?

Spiritual Capital

Will you and your family attend church? If so, what criteria will determine where you attend?

What role will God and faith play in your life?

Are you willing to commit time to building a deeper faith?

Furthermore, the buck stops with you in dealing *responsively* with life experiences over which you have little or no control. What will you do when things go wrong or don't turn out as you planned? How will you handle a job layoff, a financial setback, a serious illness or injury to you or a family member, the death of a parent or close friend, or a crisis of faith? Will you meet those experiences head-on and make the most of them, or will you wither as they rob your life of joy and vitality? The health of your experience portfolio hinges on how well you grapple with the surprising and sometimes unpleasant experiences life throws at you.

Settling Old Accounts

During the framework phase you have the opportunity to "audit" your experience portfolio by revisiting and correcting some of the early transactions. In the foundation phase—especially during your childhood and youth, most of your life experiences happened *to* you because adults made decisions about your life. Some of those experiences were painful and debilitating. Back then, you didn't know how to respond to the pain and find the path to healing. You were just a kid, so you took the blows and your experience portfolio suffered the loss.

Now you can go back to the books and try to correct some of the mistakes made in your life by other people.

79

For example, let's say that you were emotionally abandoned as a child by your father. He gave you little or none of the affection, attention, affirmation, or applause everyone needs from their father. Instead he was critical, hurtful, and hateful toward you. And you transitioned into adulthood with this huge emotional debit in your life.

You can't undo what your father did, and you may not be able to change your father's attitude or actions toward you. But you do have the right and the power to deal with the pain he caused you. You can seek professional counseling to help you work through issues of abandonment. You can decide to forgive your father, whether he seeks it or not, whether he is alive or not. If your father is still alive, you can seek to establish a positive relationship with him. And by taking such steps, you will begin to turn that debit in your experience portfolio into a credit.

Then there are the wrongs you committed as a child or youth, unresolved wrongs that left a blot on your experience portfolio. You stole something or broke something and never atoned for it. You hurt someone and didn't make it right. Whatever they were, some of the bad things you did in your wild and crazy days as a child left you with a guilty conscience as an adult. And it's difficult to accumulate true personal wealth under a cloud of guilt.

It might be impossible for you to go back and fix everything you messed up. But it may be possible for you to make some apologies or provide restitution in some circumstances. And even if you can't resolve every conflict or fix everything you've broken, you can deal with your troubled conscience. For example, a minister or spiritual counselor can help you find God's forgiveness and change unproductive behavior patterns.

The Sky's the Limit

The framework phase is also when we establish personal goals for success and dreams for happiness. We set our sights on a prestigious job, a corner office, a happy family, a dream house, a cabin by the lake, travel and adventure, close friendships, and so on. At the end of the rainbow, we envision financial security and a comfortable retirement. The framework phase includes the process of achieving our goals and realizing our dreams as much as possible.

The great pitfall in this phase is the self-imposed pressure of instant success. We charge into the grown-up world ready to grab life by the horns. We see the status, achievements, and possessions our parents and other elders enjoy and say, "That's what I want—and I want it now!" We reason, *If my company doesn't advance me fast enough, I'll switch to a company where I can climb the ladder faster.* Or we decide, *If I can't get all the toys I want before maxing out my credit card, I'll just get another card.* And our go-for-the-gusto, instant-credit, no-payments-till-next-year culture constantly encourages this attitude.

We fail to see that achieving great success is usually a process that takes years of putting in time, working hard, climbing the ladder, and earning our stripes. We must learn to enjoy each step of the journey instead of always focusing on the prizes at the end. True personal wealth is the result of embracing all of life's experiences and struggles in order to deposit them for profit in our experience portfolio.

How do you adopt this attitude? You must focus on progress, not perfection. Instead of lamenting what you don't have, what you haven't achieved, and how far you have yet to go, celebrate what you do possess, what you have achieved, and how far you've already come. Reduced to the basics, the key to the framework phase is to make a plan, work the plan, celebrate the victories, and learn from the setbacks. If you're always focused on the pot of gold at the end of the rainbow, you may miss the many valuable nuggets at your feet as you walk the path.

Phase Three — Finish Work
Early Sixties to Life's End

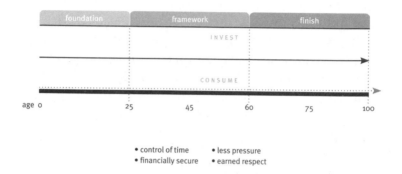

Phase three should be the most productive and enjoyable phase of life for a number of reasons.

First, you have greater control of your time. The kids are grown and gone, so you are free from the schedule demands of daily child care, school activities, soccer games, and music lessons. You may have grandchildren to love, enjoy, and at times care for. But the responsibility is not nearly so great and the amount of time you invest is at your discretion.

Furthermore, if you are a career person, you have likely reached a level of seniority that allows you to spend less time at the office or shop and more time in activities of your choosing. You have earned four or more weeks of vacation each year. You have the freedom to take personal days off here and there when you want to. And you stand at the threshold of retirement, with all the time in the world for what you want to do.

Second, you have likely achieved a degree of financial security that affords you a more comfortable lifestyle. You probably have more "fun money" in your pocket than during the previous phases. And combined with greater amounts of free time, your financial advantages may translate into the trips, cruises, and other leisure-time activities you have postponed in earlier years.

Third, and even more valuable to some people, the finish work phase promises less pressure than the earlier years of parenting and career building. Even after your children reach adulthood and independence, you never stop being a mom or dad. But you no longer have the pressure of daily care. And you may not be finished climbing the corporate ladder, but the pressure of the last rung or two is not as taxing as it was nearer the ground level.

Fourth, in the finish work phase you enjoy in greater measure the respect of others around you. You have put in your time, earned your stripes, and made significant contributions in your world. People look up to you. As the biblical proverb states, "Gray hair is a crown of splendor; it is attained by a righteous life."[1]

Fifth, you bring into the finish work phase a full portfolio of life experiences from which you can draw. You have been to the school of hard knocks and earned a master's degree. You are streetwise and experience-rich. You have a point of reference for handling most things that come your way. You have a wealth of practical learning to help you solve problems and provide advice and encouragement to others.

Here are a few important questions to consider as you anticipate the finish work phase in your life.

How Will You Handle a Life of Leisure?

The key to your success during the finish work phase is how you view and manage your transition into retirement from career, homemaking, and parenting. You will face a couple of critical decisions, and your choices will reveal whether you embrace the traditional cultural model of retirement or a unique retirement model reflecting your individual goals and values.

First, *as you approach retirement, are you focusing on working less or on working smarter and with greater zeal in your areas of interest and unique ability?* Ideally, the closer you get to retirement, the more absorbed and involved you are in your passion. The homestretch of your life's main activity—be it a career, parenting and grandparenting, community service, a home-based business—should be the most exciting and fulfilling. As you head for the finish line, are you limping and complaining or charging down the homestretch having the time of your life?

Second, *when you reach retirement age, will you simply jettison all responsibilities and ride off into the sunset, or will you launch into a new and exciting adventure?* In other words, is your mentality to retire *from* something or *to* something? Is retirement the end or another, more exciting beginning? Life expectancy for retirees who just check out of work to do nothing is only about eight years. People who lose their sense of value and purpose in life don't last very long. Dr. Howard Hendricks said it this way: "The day your past becomes more exciting than your future is the day you begin to die."[2]

What Will You Leave Behind?

The finish work phase ends with your death. Even though your body will be laid to rest, some things from

84

your time here on earth will live on. Your legacy consists of at least three elements.

Finances and material possessions. Have you heard the joke about the shortest will ever written? The punch line goes something like, "I, being of sound mind, spent it all." Or perhaps you have seen the bumper sticker on one of those big RVs: "We're spending our kids' inheritance." Some people have that mentality. Since they can't take it with them, they're doing their best to use up their resources before they die.

But most people don't approach life's end that way. They want to leave something tangible behind—an inheritance of cash, property, and possessions for their children; an endowment for their alma mater; a significant contribution to charity; or some combination of benevolent acts.

Depending on your level of financial success during your lifetime, you may or may not be able to leave a substantial amount of money and/or goods behind for others. No matter what kind of financial legacy survives you, you will definitely leave behind your values and attitudes about money and possessions. Your healthy attitude toward money can be an even greater blessing to your beneficiaries than the dollar amount you bequeath them.

Impact. What will people say about you when you're gone—"great loss" or "good riddance"? What will be their choicest memories of the life you lived—your compassion and helpfulness or your sour and obstinate nature? What words will they use to describe you—"loving spouse," "devoted parent," "selfless," "selfish," "absent"? The answers to these questions reveal the legacy of impact you will leave behind.

Influence. Your greatest potential for a rich legacy is in the area of your influence. In order to determine the level of influence you will have, you must answer this question: How will your family members, friends, coworkers, neighbors, and others be different as a result of having known you? It's not just how people remember you that determines your legacy; it's how you influenced them—hopefully for the better. Will your children live as fine, upstanding citizens because of what you taught and modeled? Will your work associates be inspired and better equipped for their tasks for having worked alongside you? Will your example of generosity leave numbers of generous people in its wake? Will your devotion to God have encouraged others to trust him with their lives?

Influence is so important to acquiring true personal wealth that I will discuss it in greater detail in the next chapter.

How Will Your "Life Sentence" End?

Have you ever wandered through a cemetery reading headstones? Most of them bear a name and two dates—birth and death. Some include a few words or a sentence summarizing the deceased's life, such as "Our Baby," "Precious Wife and Mother," "A Saint in This World, an Angel in the Next."

Someday a brief summary will be written on your headstone. You are not only composing your "life sentence" as you live, you are determining the extent of your legacy.

Alfred Nobel, nineteenth-century scientist, received a wake-up call that motivated him to do something about the legacy he would leave. Early in his career, Nobel invented dynamite, intended as an aid to construction and progress. But, of course, what one person intends for good, others employ for evil. Dynamite became responsible for the death of many people.

When Alfred Nobel's brother died in 1888, it was mistakenly reported in the newspapers that Alfred Nobel had died.

A premature obituary summarized his life in these words: Alfred Nobel . . . Merchant of Death. Nobel was taken aback that the world would remember him primarily for his destructive invention. So over the next several years he threw his energies into creating the Nobel Peace Prize.

You have the same opportunity regarding your legacy.

Where are you on the time line I have described? Are you in the foundation phase, heady with independence and brimming with optimism for the future? Are you somewhere in the framework phase, building a family and career, chasing your goals and dreams? Or are you in the finish work phase, closer to the end than to the beginning?

Now, how would you characterize the bottom line of your experience portfolio at this point in your life? Are you rich with the many varied experiences you have deposited? Have you learned how to transform bad or painful experiences into assets in your life? Or are you feeling destitute, having missed many opportunities by assuming that true wealth is all about you and what you can accumulate?

No matter where you are at this moment or what your bottom line looks like, you can set out on the path to true personal wealth.

Small Change *Challenges*

- In this chapter, I talked about focusing on the progress you have made rather than lamenting what you haven't achieved and measuring your success against perfection. This is an attitude that must be learned and a habit that must be practiced. Over the next thirty days, end each day by making a list of at least five positive results or progress made for that day. Tell yourself every day, *It's about progress, not perfection!*

6

The Road to True Personal Wealth

————————•————————

The destination is true personal wealth, to experience throughout life increasing levels of satisfaction, fulfillment, and enjoyment in all areas of personal experience: financial, relational, physical, intellectual, and spiritual. The ultimate payoff is your legacy, what you leave behind after your death—not only financial and material acquisitions but a significant, positive influence on others. The vital question is "How can I reach that destination and realize that rich payoff as I journey through the foundation, framework, and finish phases of my life?" In other words, how will you vector toward this most desirable outcome? You need to know how you can get from where you are today to where you want to be at life's end.

People tend to travel three different paths throughout life: the path of indifference, the path of indulgence, and the path of influence. Only one of these paths leads to true personal wealth. The other two, though well-traveled by many, lead to personal bankruptcy. No one sticks to one path exclusively; we all spend at least a little time on each. But as we journey through the three phases of life, every one of us tends to gravitate toward one of these paths as the major thoroughfare for his or her life.

The path of life you currently travel may not be a conscious choice on your part. You may simply respond to the "herd instinct," trudging along in the same direction those around you seem to be heading. Or you may have been strongly influenced onto your life path by the example and admonition of parents or other significant influences. But in the final analysis, the path you travel is your choice. As you read this chapter, if you discover that you are heading in the wrong direction, you can choose to change direction and set a course to acquire true personal wealth.

The Path of Indifference:
An Existence-Centered Life

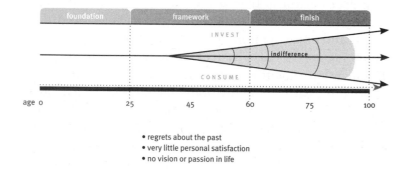

- regrets about the past
- very little personal satisfaction
- no vision or passion in life

Claire is only thirty-eight years old, but she has already given up on life. Nothing has gone the way she had hoped, so she has switched to autopilot. She endures a marriage virtually devoid of love, intimacy, excitement, and hope. She "settled" for Ernie because he had fathered their only child while they were dating. And now that Tanya is off to college, Claire has little to live for. Hers is a life of regret and constant disappointment.

Having been born during the Great Depression, Jake and Alma spent their lives hoarding their money in fear of the stark poverty their parents endured. Jake worked hard for more than forty years at a job he despised. He made good money, but the couple scrimped and saved like paupers. They lived week to week just to pay the bills, keep the pantry stocked with canned goods, and fill the tank with gas. Paranoid that they would not have enough to live on in retirement, they put everything else into savings. Now approaching their eighties, Jake and Alma have little to show for their lives beyond the bank account they will never deplete nor fully enjoy.

Randall, age twenty-nine, is a loner. He doesn't date because dating could lead to marriage, and he doesn't want the responsibility of a wife and family. Hating the office politics and games where he was employed, Randall started his own at-home business so he could work without being bothered. He only earns about half what he used to, but it's worth it to him to be out of the rat race. Randall has no close friends because friends are more trouble than they're worth. Friends always need something, and Randall doesn't want to be needed. His motto is "Leave me alone to do my own thing."

Claire, Jake and Alma, and Randall are all at different places on the path of indifference. People vectoring in this direction don't find much satisfaction in anything. They have little vision or passion for life. They just want to get through the day, the week, the month. Work and finances are only a means to exist. Relationships are of value only when they help the existence-centered person get through life. Religious faith is regarded as an exercise to help them hang on. Life is not so much to enjoy as to endure.

Many people end up on the path of indifference because negative life experiences depleted their portfolio, leaving them regretful and apathetic. Instead of trying to turn these negative experiences into credits by dealing with them, they live to avoid more bad experiences in the future. Instead of extending themselves to seek and embrace positive experiences, they work hard just to maintain the status quo. And yet "life inflation"—unavoidable difficulties and pains in life that affect everyone—continues to drain their portfolio, leading to bankruptcy.

The path of indifference is the "default setting." Notice on the graphic that this path just shoots straight down the middle with no alteration in course. The path of indifference is the one you will most likely travel if you just let life happen to you without taking an active role in where you're going. Sure, we all experience periods or seasons when we respond to life indifferently. But the existence-centered person camps on this path as a way of life.

The Path of Indulgence: A Self-Centered Life

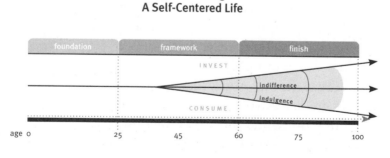

- "I've put in my time and paid my dues"
- personal satisfaction from prestige & possessions
- narrow perspective of life

92

When Donald finished his stint with the navy following the Korean conflict, he moved his wife, Ellie, and his infant daughter from the Midwest, where they were raised, to San Diego, California, where he had been stationed. He got a job as a ditchdigger with the water department, determined to work hard, advance, and soar above the near-poverty-level existence he and Ellie had known as kids. And Donald's hard work paid off. Over the years he rose through the ranks to achieve the highest position available to him without a college degree: senior field supervisor.

Along the way, he and Ellie had two more kids. When all three kids were in school, she took a job as a market clerk. Early on they had mapped out a plan for both of them to retire in their midfifties so they could travel the country in their RV. Donald's goal was to fish and play golf in every state in the union. So the couple lived frugally and saved diligently to reach their goal. Their narrow focus and determination kept them from many activities with their growing number of grandchildren.

They retired right on schedule with a nest egg more than adequate to fulfill their dream. By that time they had seven grandchildren, all living in Southern California. But Donald and Ellie had worked hard for this moment, and they weren't going to squander it hanging around home. They had put in their time raising their own kids, and now it was their time. They bought a large RV, rented out their home, and headed off for their retirement adventure.

Donald and Ellie barely knew their grandchildren before they took off to tour the country. They had been too absorbed in their goal to invest much time in the kids. Their departure from Southern California all but ended any possibility of a close relationship. Over the next thirteen years, Donald and Ellie were gone more than they were home. And when they *were* home, they were either too tired from their journey or too involved in preparing another trip to be bothered with the kids or grandkids. Then Donald dropped dead of a heart attack, still fourteen states short of his goal. Ellie died two years later. Three of their seven grandkids, all young adults by this time, didn't even attend the funeral.

The path of indulgence is a conscious choice to live for yourself instead of for others. This is one of two ways to step away from the path of indifference, and many in our culture opt for this path. The operative word for the self-indulgent lifestyle is *consume*. These individuals derive personal satisfaction from pleasure, possessions, power, and prestige. They center their life experiences on acquiring, owning, and consuming things and people rather than investing in others.

Donald and Ellie chose a life of indulgence, pouring all their attention and energies into preparing for and enjoying their retirement. Life was all about them, not their kids or grandkids. They didn't live extravagantly, nor did they spend much time or money on entertainment. Rather, they were focused on their own interests and amusements, which left little time for others.

The self-centered life can take other forms of indulgence and consumption. Francine is too intent on making her mark in the male-dominated corporate world to think about long-term relationships of any kind. She won't allow herself to get close to anyone because she doesn't want a friendship or romance to delay her rise to the top.

Brad is a workaholic also, but he is driven by the money he can earn and the things he can buy. He is a techno junkie, forever searching out state-of-the-art computers and home theater equipment. He relates only to people who are into what he's into.

Now, don't confuse *indulgence* and *consumption* with *enjoyment*. Nothing is wrong with making money, having possessions, and living life to the fullest. Delighting in the fruits of our labor is reasonable and justifiable. Having a well-thought-out plan for retirement is wise and prudent. Working hard, taking on greater responsibility, and enjoying the resulting recognition and prestige are fine. You can enjoy life and its pleasures and rewards without being indulgent. It boils down to the attitude of the heart. If all you live for is to acquire, enjoy, and consume without regard for anyone or anything else, you're hurtling down the path of self-indulgence. You may end up with a net financial worth rivaling a small country. But if your experience portfolio is bereft of relational, physical, intellectual, and spiritual capital, you will be personally bankrupt.

The consuming individual uses money to get what he wants in order to lavish it on himself. Work goals center on financial rewards, personal advancement, recognition, importance, perks, prestige, and power. Relationships are primarily forged, maintained, or dissolved for selfish means. Those who help me get what I want are courted; those who don't are ignored. Proficiencies are developed and exercised for maximum reward; I'll employ whatever skills bring me the greatest return. As for spiritual capital, the self-centered person rejects or minimizes any god or religious experience that interferes with me-first pursuits.

The mantra on the path of self-indulgence is "I want it; I deserve it; I will have it; don't get in my way." Entering the finish stage of life, this person asserts, "I have put in my time and paid my dues. Leave me alone to enjoy my rewards." The self-centered person squanders life experiences and relationships, and no amount of money, position, or power can compensate for such consumption.

When I think of the person vectoring down the path of indulgence, I am reminded of the humorous view of the life of a toddler, summarized in the "Toddler's Creed":

If I want it, it's mine.
If I give it to you and change my mind later, it's mine.
If I can take it away from you, it's mine.
If I had it a little while ago, it's still mine.
If it's mine, it will never belong to anyone else no matter what.
If we are building something together, all the pieces are mine.
If it looks just like mine, it is mine![1]

If you have toddlers at home, you know what I'm talking about. In fact, if you have teenagers at home, you know what I'm talking about, don't you? The sad truth is that many people today buy into the lie of our culture that life is all about getting what you want. You deserve to get all you can, so go for it regardless of how it impacts others. Without realizing it, we embrace the Toddler's Creed as adults, setting us on the path of indulgence.

The Path of Influence:
An Others-Centered Life

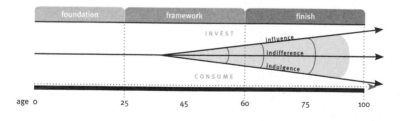

• transformation of others
• personal satisfaction seeing others benefit
• broader perspective of life

At first glance, you might think Ned lives a life of indulgence. At sixty-eight, he and his wife of forty-two years, Betty, are living the life of their dreams. Having worked hard and invested wisely, Ned and Betty are enjoying the fruits of their labor. They take at least one cruise and a couple of other big trips every year. Ned bought season tickets to his hometown NBA team, and he and Betty eat out at least three times a week. Over the last two years, they have completely redecorated their home—new furnishings, floors, draperies. They are living the high life.

But you also need to know that Ned and Betty invite one of their seven grandchildren along every time they take a trip. Their grandkids are getting a firsthand education in geography as they travel the country and the world with Grandma and Grandpa. And the couple relishes these times for making each child feel special.

Ned is also mentoring a group of young men from his church, and he uses his NBA tickets as a means to get together with one or two of them and encourage them to be devoted husbands and fathers. Ned and Betty also volunteer at a senior center, arranging programs and scheduling the Meals on Wheels team. And every summer, Ned sponsors one or two underprivileged students at the inner-city sports camp he helps organize.

Ned and Betty are traveling the path of influence. They are having a great time, but the focus of their lives since the early years of their marriage has been on others. Not only does their financial portfolio overflow from careful spending and wise decisions, their experience portfolio overflows as they use what they have acquired and what they have learned to help others. They have come to experience the words of legendary basketball coach John Wooden: "Real happiness and success comes from things that cannot be taken from you."[2]

97

Others-centered individuals derive their primary satisfaction and fulfillment from seeing other people benefit and grow. In one sense you may say they are merely giving back to the community what they have received. But others-centered people don't view it as a debt to be paid. They choose to invest their resources, energy, skills, and wisdom in others in order to see them transformed.

Those vectoring down the path of influence look at every life experience as an opportunity to influence people in a positive way. You will hear them say such things as, "I'm interested in you. I have something to offer. I am committed to your well-being and growth as a person."

Here's what the path of influence might look like in the five areas of personal wealth capital.

Financial capital. Carl is a radiology technician at a medical clinic in his rural community. He makes a decent living for himself and his wife, Connie. The couple lives even more modestly than they need to because they are committed to sharing what they have with others in need. Specifically, Carl and Connie take great joy in helping some of the ministers in their small town meet financial needs.

One time, Carl learned that the poorly paid minister of a small church needed a second car in order to keep up with his visits to church members. The family minivan was a gas-guzzler and left the minister's wife and kids without transportation when he was out. Carl approached the minister and asked if a second car would be helpful. The minister said, "Yes, but it's not something we can afford."

"Well," Carl said, "Your colleague Reverend Judd at the Community Church has an older VW bug for sale. It's not much to look at, but it runs like a top and is very easy on gas. If you think it would meet your need, Connie and I would like to buy it for you. We believe in what you're doing, and we would be privileged to help in this small way."

The minister was dumbfounded at the offer. He humbly accepted, and within a week he was in the old VW on his frequent trips to the hospital and local rest homes to visit parishioners. The minister used the car for several years, then passed it on to someone else in the same spirit of generosity.

People of influence are interested in investing their money and resources in the betterment of others. These people give generously—even sacrificially at times—to help the less fortunate, to support worthy causes, or to meet a financial or material need for someone. They don't do it out of duty or constraint. They do it because they find it even more fulfilling and satisfying than spending the money on themselves. They are the people of whom it was written, "God loves a cheerful giver."[3]

Relational capital. The apostle Paul instructed, "The things you have heard me say in the presence of many witnesses entrust to reliable men who will also be qualified to teach others."[4] There is a significant relational principle in these words: Invest what you are and what you have learned in those around you so they can do the same for others. This facet of the life of influence has many applications. Here are a few examples:

- Senior citizens with free time volunteer to read to children at the local school.
- A mature couple with a strong marriage offers to mentor young couples on relational skills.
- A business executive reads extensively and attends conferences in his field in order to be a knowledgeable resource for the employees he is training.

- A single woman gives ten hours a week at the local hospital.
- A family man purposely schedules weekly date nights with his wife and one-on-one activities with each of his children.
- A family "adopts" an elderly, shut-in neighbor lady, visiting her often, running errands for her, and helping her with household chores.
- Retired grandparents leave the community they love and move across country to be near their four grandchildren and to be a positive influence for them.
- A foreman spends time after work with an apprentice, giving extra instruction and offering encouragement.

Physical capital. Two girlfriends met for lunch. Lynn noticed that Andrea ordered a small, nutritious meal. "Andy," Lynn said, "you already look great. You don't need to lose any weight. Why are you eating like you're on a crash diet?"

"I'm staying in shape for the wedding," Andrea said.

"Whose wedding?" Lynn said. "Your kids aren't even teenagers yet."

"Actually, I'm staying in shape for my grandkids' wedding," Andrea said with a twinkle in her eye. "I plan to be there for every one of them and dance till midnight."

If you fail to maintain your physical, emotional, and mental health, you will have less to offer others than if you keep yourself in all-around good health. By maintaining your health, you will live longer and have more strength and energy for a life of influence with those around you.

Intellectual capital. Doug found a software program on the Internet that helped him streamline his paperwork, leaving more time for telephone sales calls. He was salesperson of the month for three months straight. Wendy, another member of the sales staff, approached him one day. "Doug, you're setting new sales records. What's your secret?"

For many people, the work environment is marked by competition, suspicion, and a territorial mind-set. If you give your coworker too much help, he or she may be promoted ahead of you. If you train your subordinates too well, they could take your job. Others-centered workers don't see it this way. They realize that they are where they are because others trained them, taught them, or otherwise helped them get there. They are generous to share knowledge, skills, and tricks of the trade. Benefiting others is a higher priority than personal gain.

Understanding this principle, Doug responded, "Oh, it's no secret. Let me show you a little trick I learned recently," as he showed Wendy the software program.

Spiritual capital. Tom read carefully the brochure he had picked up at church regarding a workshop on prayer. "Could this help me in my pursuit of a closer relationship with God?" He knew the workshop would take another night of his busy schedule, but he filled out the registration form and sent it in without hesitation.

The others-centered individual is open to the prospect of God's existence and claims on his or her life. God is a person—an "other." To be others-centered is to endeavor to know him and relate to him. We don't seek to know God in order to influence him, of course. Rather, we approach God to be influenced by him so that we may positively influence others.

Cautions on the Path of Influence

A couple of guardrails on the path of influence will keep you on the road.

1. Don't confuse influence with mere activity or busyness.
Many of us cram our calendars full of activities: family,
friends, work, church, civic groups, social events. But why
do we do what we do? Is it to fill the time, avoid other
tasks, or stave off boredom? Do we enter into activities for
personal satisfaction, attention, or applause? That's not
a life of influence; that's a life of busyness and personal
pursuit. Some days I feel as if I have done nothing but
spin my wheels. I come home wondering, *What did I really accomplish?* I was busy, but the results were less than
stellar. Those are usually the days when my time was spent
in activities that were definitely outside my strengths and
the opportunity to contribute to others.

The question we must ask ourselves about every activity
is "Am I doing the best I can with the opportunity at hand
to positively influence, help, and encourage those around
me?" There may be activities in which your influence is
minimal, ignored, or unwanted. There may be situations
that don't warrant significant influence. But the key is your
alertness and preparation to serve others in any situation
as the need arises.

*2. Don't try to measure the effectiveness of your influence
by comparing yourself to others.* You have a unique "sphere
of influence," which encompasses all the people with whom
you are in contact. Every person's sphere of influence is
different. Some are very large because those individuals
interact with hundreds or perhaps thousands of people.
Your sphere of influence may be smaller. It's not the size
of your sphere of influence that is important; it's what you
do to impact those within your unique sphere.

Let me illustrate with two individuals, Kayla and Desmond. Kayla heads up a national ministry to women. She
speaks at conferences all across the country. She has a
national cable television program. She has written several

books on marriage and women's issues. Kayla's sphere of influence is huge.

Desmond is a single, slightly mentally handicapped school janitor who works swing shift. He lives alone and has no real friends. But since he doesn't have to start work until 4:00 P.M., every day he walks two blocks from his small apartment to the nursing home. There he spends an hour visiting with the three male patients in the home. Desmond is not a profound conversationalist, but neither are his three old buddies. Desmond likes to bring them candy treats, sit with them, tell jokes, and occasionally help them get comfortable. Desmond's sphere of influence is quite small.

Both Kayla and Desmond effectively help and encourage people within their spheres of influence. It's not important how many people you influence but what you contribute to the people within your sphere.

Another danger of comparison is in the area of what you do. You may look at others around you and disqualify yourself because you are not as smart or gifted or skilled as others. For example, someone like Desmond might be tempted to discount his contribution to others because it's not as impressive as Kayla's. Kayla has a Ph.D., she can speak, she can write, she puts marriages back together, she leads a large organization. Desmond visits three old guys at the nursing home.

You not only have a unique sphere of influence, you have a package of specific abilities and skills. You are a composite of your personality, your God-given abilities, your education, your temperament, your interests, your experiences, and your passions. Nobody else in the world is put together like you. At the core of who you are is your unique ability, that collection of things you do very well and enjoy doing tremendously. I sometimes refer to unique ability as your "sweet spot," a passion so deep and so real that when you're involved in it, you find yourself exulting, "This is what I'm made for!"

Your greatest satisfaction on the path of influence will come as you serve people in the way you are wired. Desmond would feel ill-equipped, uncomfortable, and defeated trying do what Kayla does. Kayla would feel the same way in Desmond's shoes. And you will fare no better trying to be somebody you're not. The people in your world need what you have to offer. True personal wealth results as you exercise your unique ability in a way that benefits those around you. We will talk more about discovering your unique ability in the chapters ahead.

❖

As a member of the speaking team for an organization called FamilyLife, I occasionally attend retreats where we are equipped for a new season of conferences. A few years back, Dr. and Mrs. Howard Hendricks were invited to the retreat to encourage and motivate the more than fifty couples attending. Dr. Hendricks has had a remarkable teaching career, influencing and helping train thousands of men and women who are in ministry around the world. Dr. and Mrs. Hendricks were in their late-seventies and into their second fifty years of marriage when they came to our retreat.

One morning, Dr. and Mrs. Hendricks sat on the auditorium platform in two overstuffed chairs for a question-and-answer session. The hundred or so in the audience were respected Christian leaders and gifted communicators in their own right. But they sat on the edge of their seats, hoping to glean every ounce of wisdom and insight from a couple who had lived a life of influence.

That time with Dr. and Mrs. Hendricks was a defining moment for me. As I listened to them, I thought, *That's what I want! What better way to finish my life than to know I lived in such a way that others were interested in what I had to say. How rewarding it would be to realize that others crave the wisdom of my years and find encouragement and help for their lives in my experiences. How satisfying to share the riches of my true personal wealth right up to my last breath.*

I don't want to just take up space. I don't want to just put in my seventy, eighty, or ninety years and be the subject of a nice obituary. I don't want to just grab all the gusto I can and say with the Frank Sinatra song, "I did it my way." I want my years on earth to mean something. I want to live a life of integrity, work hard, and invest in others in such a way that, even when I am pushing eighty, I have a deep reservoir of wisdom, ideas, counsel, and advice people will draw from. And I believe many of you share my desire. That's why I have chosen to walk the path of influence.

But that kind of finish doesn't just happen. It's a journey of acquiring true personal wealth by living a life of influence. And the sooner you vector your life onto the path of influence, the richer will be your reward of true personal wealth at journey's end.

What path are you traveling? Are you marking time, treading water, ambling through life aimlessly and indifferently? Perhaps you are charging down the path of indulgence collecting all the stuff, pleasures, and acclaim you can grab. The very best you can hope for from a life of indifference or indulgence isn't even on the radar screen in comparison to the rich personal reward experienced on the path of influence.

No matter which phase of life you're in and no matter how far you may have wandered down the path of indif-

ference or indulgence, you can make a vector change. We'll
see how in the next chapter.

Small Change *Challenges*

- Which of the three paths—indifference, indulgence,
  and influence—do you find yourself traveling most
  of the time?
- Make a list of all the spheres of influence in which
  you find yourself.
- What is one specific thing you could commit to
  today that would enhance your ability to influence
  others?

7

The Vector Principle

———————•———————

A man was born in New York in the early 1700s who, for obvious reasons, I will refer to as William Smith. Smith was a godless man of no principle, and he married a woman of like character. This couple did not choose a life of influence. Rather, they spent their lives in indulgence and consumption. What was the result? Among twelve hundred of the Smiths' known descendants who were studied, we find this assortment of characters:

- 1026 descendants
- 300 convicts
- 27 were murderers
- 190 prostitutes
- 509 alcoholics and drug addicts[1]

None of William Smith's descendants made a significant contribution to society. Rather, collectively this family cost the state of New York millions of dollars.

Contrast the life and impact of Smith with another man born around the same time. Jonathan Edwards was a minister and theologian, a man of upstanding character. He married a woman who shared his values and commitment to live a life of positive influence. A study of some of their descendants reveals these amazing results:

- 929 descendants
- 430 ministers
- 314 war veterans
- 75 authors
- 86 college professors
- 13 university presidents
- 7 congressmen
- 3 governors
- 1 vice president of the United States[2]

What was the difference between these two men? True, they may have been influenced by others in the direction their lives turned, but neither of them was forced to take a particular path of life. As young men, they both had the opportunity to determine the course of their lives, to choose indulgence, indifference, or influence. It's as if they stood shoulder to shoulder at a fork in the road. For whatever reasons, Smith took the low road and Edwards took the high road.

In the early years of the journey, the two paths these men took may not have been very far apart. But as the years rolled by, the distance increased. As the two lists above testify, succeeding generations found themselves a world apart. And it all began with a few simple choices.

Changing Direction, Setting a New Course

This phenomenon illustrates how the Vector Principle operates, with both positive and negative outcomes. The direction of your life at this moment has been influenced by the choices you have made over the past months, years, and even decades of your life. Those small and seemingly insignificant decisions may be vectoring you toward the life you want or heading you in a different and painful direction.

For example, let's say that as a child you stole a candy bar from a store like I did. But your dad didn't catch you and make you pay for it, and you overcame the pangs of your conscience. Perhaps it even gave you a thrill to steal something and get away with it. That could have been a slight vector change in a bad direction.

In no way am I inferring that you are destined for a life of crime and a future in prison because you stole a candy bar as a kid. But at the very least, that vector away from a life of influence is steering you in the direction of personal bankruptcy. And who knows how your poor choices will negatively affect your kids and grandkids. Turn around and see who's following you down the path you're taking.

Look at William Smith. He never set out to be the patriarch of such a motley line of criminals and ne'er-do-wells. But his early choices to serve self, indulge, and consume vectored him in the direction of a life of pain, misery, and fruitlessness. His example apparently impacted the choices of his children, grandchildren, and generations beyond.

Similarly, Jonathan Edwards may not have envisioned the generation-to-generation ramifications of his early choices to serve God and invest his life in people. But his vector change toward a life of influence impacted not only his family but our nation in countless significant and lasting ways.

Trickle-Down Influence

I call it "trickle-down influence"—the ripple effect of our life choices on others around us. Every decision you make, every action you take, and every attitude you hold affects the people within your sphere of influence. When your life reverberates positively, others pick up on it and are encouraged to replicate it. You know how a cold or the flu can spread through the family or the office just because people are in close proximity? It's sort of that way with trickle-down influence—only in a good sense. People "catch" positive attitudes and helpful actions.

Brian has been married for eight years and has three young sons. Part of Brian's vector change to a life of influence involved starting each day by reading from the Bible. An early riser, Brian would sit down at the kitchen table every morning for his time of devotions while his wife and sons slept. Occasionally one of the boys woke up early, wandered into the kitchen, and saw Dad sitting with an open Bible. Brian never made a big deal of it, but the boys noticed.

One morning when the boys were teenagers, Brian walked into the kitchen with his Bible to find that his seat was taken. One of his sons was sitting at the table reading his own Bible. Brian never told him to do it. The lad was simply the beneficiary of trickle-down influence. He had learned a good thing simply by watching his dad do a good thing. Today all three of Brian's sons are married and serving God just like their dad. And Brian's example of godliness continues to trickle down through his boys to others.

Here's a different example of trickle-down influence, one in which the influence was more "programmed" than in Brian's case.

After my financial wake-up call as a young husband, the time Nancy threw the checkbook at me, we began to budget our money and watch our spending. We literally started with the envelope system. Nancy and I ran a tight financial ship, and soon we had the hang of it. This financial victory brought us greater financial security. We were able to give more money away, which increased our sense of satisfaction and fulfillment in life.

But it didn't stop with us. We consciously decided to make sure that what we had learned trickled down to our kids. We began to teach them the same financial disciplines when they became freshmen in high school. I figured out about how much we spent on them each month for things like entertainment, clothing, and gas and then paid them that amount in two monthly installments. They became responsible to meet their own needs with the money I gave them.

They struggled with this plan at first. And when they blew their wad, I held a hard line. They were not allowed to tap into the ATM machine named Dad until their next scheduled payday. In time they began to manage their finances with great skill. In addition to budgeting the money that we gave them, they began to work, earn their own money, and save for longer-term goals. When our kids entered college, they each bought their own cars and paid for their own insurance. We are now reaping the benefits of teaching them what we learned when we made a vector change in the management of our finances before they were born.

The Domino Effect

A vector change in one dimension of your portfolio can create a positive domino effect in other dimensions. For example, say Susan decides to see a financial planner and get serious about establishing and operating within a budget. For the first time in her life, she actually has a handle on where her money is going. Many times, a little knowledge is the beginning of positive changes. Now Susan can begin to allocate some of her discretionary funds to a long-term investment account. It feels good and creates peace of mind. She is emotionally healthier as a result of her financial decision.

Susan's improving finances allow her to join a health club. She begins to work out regularly, and she feels better physically. Since she has more energy and drive, she signs up for that photography class she always wanted to take. It blossoms into a full-fledged hobby. A teenager down the street watches Susan take pictures and is full of questions about cameras. She begins to coach her on the skills of photography she has learned in class. They spend a few hours each weekend taking pictures together and printing them at home.

This opens up a whole new world for that young person. She goes on to college and majors in the fine arts with an emphasis on photography. She eventually lands a wonderful job with *National Geographic* and wins a Pulitzer prize for a photo essay on a third-world country.

Sound a little far-fetched? This example is fiction, but I hear story after story of people encouraged to greatness by an unsuspecting "influencer" who made a small vector change that produced a compounding effect. Why is it so hard for us to imagine that we can influence others to happiness and greatness?

112

Vector Changes through Life's Phases

Let's look at how a vector change can affect each of the three phases of life: foundation, framework, and finish.

Vectoring in the Foundation Phase

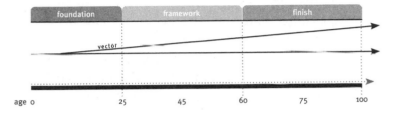

The foundation phase is the easiest time to vector toward a life of influence. Youth and young adulthood is the time for setting life goals. You don't have as much baggage to deal with. You're not set in your ways. Your experience portfolio is not so burdened with debt that you cannot adjust. Indeed, if you have a parent or another strong influence like Brian, you may even be predisposed toward true personal wealth as a result of trickle-down influence. And if you have already started down the path of indifference or indulgence, changing course is not a major adjustment. Notice in the graphic how small the angle is at this stage.

But even a slight vector change in the foundation phase can produce enormous results. Take the dimension of financial capital as an example. Sean and Amy are a newly married couple in their midtwenties. They have determined to live a life of influence and want to use their money and resources to help others as much as possible. But they are just getting started in their careers. They are not making much money, and they still have school loans to pay off. So their vector change in the financial dimension is very

113

small. Here are the steps Sean and Amy have decided to take:

1. Establish a budget and stick to it. This won't cost them any money, and it will certainly help them better control the money they have by minimizing impulse spending. One line item in their budget is "charitable giving." Sean and Amy decided to cut back their entertainment fund in order to give something each month to their favorite charities. It's not much, but it's a small way in which they can help others.

2. Balance the checkbook every month. This is another effort to help them keep close tabs on where every penny goes. Letting bank statements pile up unopened month to month is a good way to lose track fast.

3. Pay themselves first. They consider a savings account as one of their monthly bills to be paid right off the top. At first they can only afford ten dollars a month. This amount will increase as their salaries increase. They have also decided to divert work bonuses and other financial windfalls into the savings account. Sean and Amy are thinking six to eight years ahead when they will start a family. They plan to use their savings as a down payment on a home. Hopefully by that time Amy will be able to cut back on work to be home with their children.

4. Maximize 401(k) contributions. Both their employers offer good retirement plans. Sean and Amy cannot afford to match their employers' contributions at the outset, but they have budgeted to start in that direction with a manageable amount.

5. Give to their church. In addition to giving to charities, Sean and Amy are committed to giving a percent-

age—one-tenth, a tithe—of their income to the ministry of their church. For this couple, church giving is part of the spiritual dimension of their lives. They consider that they are giving to God, who uses their gifts through the ministry of the church to help others locally and around the world.

6. Establish a relationship with a financial planner. Sean and Amy know there will be more money to deal with as the years go by. So they are methodically interviewing a number of financial planners with a view to paying for these services in the future.

Follow Sean and Amy's small financial vector out ten years and you will see some remarkable results. They will have a significant amount of money in savings and/or equity in their house and in retirement funds. And they will have generously supported their charities and their church's ministry. As they continue to modify their original goals as their income increases, that vector change will become even more dramatic. And if they stay the course, you can imagine what their financial portfolio will look like at retirement, not to mention all the good they will have done with their resources.

But this is only one dimension of this couple's life. Imagine that Sean and Amy are just as committed to investing capital in the relational, physical, intellectual, and spiritual dimensions as in the financial. Again, small vector changes in the foundation stage will pay huge dividends of influence over the years. Here's what those initial goals might look like:

Investing Relational Capital
- Schedule a weekly date with my spouse to really talk and listen to each other.

- Schedule a quarterly, semiannual, or annual "retreat" with my spouse to do some goal review and long-term planning.
- Attend a marriage enrichment conference with my spouse once each year.
- Invite our neighbors over for dinner at least once each year.
- Get involved with a small group of young couples at church for mutual encouragement in our marriages.

Investing Physical Capital

- Schedule a physical exam and establish a baseline for personal health and fitness.
- Collect and use recipes that provide a healthy diet.
- Commit to a program of daily exercise: walking, running, swimming, tennis. Save for a treadmill.
- Avoid excessive hours of overtime and missed days off and vacations due to job demands.

Investing Intellectual Capital

- Take advantage of educational opportunities and resources offered by my employer for my training and advancement.
- Read one book each month on a subject outside my work interests and responsibility.
- Discover my unique strengths and abilities and determine ways to focus my energies in those areas.
- Spend five to ten hours a month in a helpful volunteer activity that utilizes my abilities.

Investing Spiritual Capital

- Attend church and a Bible study group regularly.
- Read the Bible fifteen minutes every day.
- Journal my spiritual thoughts, insights, and questions.
- Pray with and for my spouse every day.
- Periodically meet with a minister or spiritual counselor who can provide additional guidance for my spiritual journey.

Any person or couple who sets and follows such a vector toward a life of influence will experience the continued growth and enjoyment of true personal wealth

Vectoring in the Framework Phase

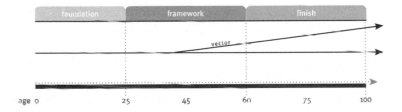

"I'm happy for young people like Sean and Amy," some may say, "but it's too late for me. I'm pushing forty (or fifty or sixty) and I've spent my life on myself. I don't think a change now can pull me out of personal poverty."

People in the financial services industry hear the same kind of argument from some of their prospective clients. As young adults these people were financially irresponsible. They spent foolishly, ran up credit card debt, and ignored sound advice to save and invest. Suddenly it hits them: They have done little to prepare for retirement, and they are afraid any efforts to correct the problem at this time will be a futile exercise in "too little too late."

Financial advisors shoot straight with them. They say, "Yes, you have missed some opportunities in the past that would have provided a much nicer outcome for you. But it's never too late to do something. If you start today you will at least have a larger portfolio than if you continue to do nothing. And the more you set aside now, the better it will be."

The same is true across all dimensions of personal wealth. The key to understanding the impact of vector changes is that small course corrections can have substantial impact if given time to work. Granted, you may have squandered some time in the past. But you have plenty of time left to make a difference. And since you likely have more equity in your experience portfolio than people like Sean and Amy who are just getting started in life, you have more leverage for vector changes and the impact becomes even more significant.

So instead of lamenting how much of your life you may have wasted, think about how much time you yet have to invest in others. The psalmist in the Bible prayed, "Teach us to number our days, that we may apply our hearts unto wisdom."[3] How many days do you have left? Current life expectancy is roughly seventy-five years for men and seventy-nine years for women. If you calculate the time you have left in days, you'll probably be amazed at the opportunities for investment still ahead of you.

As I write these words, I am forty-seven years old. I'm planning on being around at least twenty-eight more years. So I have more than ten thousand days left to live life to the fullest and make contributions of influence in my sphere of relationships.

118

If I make just a few critical vector changes right now, the impact can be huge over my remaining ten thousand–plus days. For example, think what could happen if I were to donate an additional $100 each month to a charitable cause. Over the rest of my life that contribution would amount to $129,600, given an average return of 8 percent on the investment. Imagine how much good an organization could do with $129,600!

Or let's say I decide to send one underprivileged child to a summer camp every year until I die. This decision alone could help change the lives of twenty-eight children. And if the change in those kids' lives was powerful and significant, it should positively affect the way they raise their children, which in turn may have a positive effect on the next generation. Now we're talking about influencing possibly hundreds of people.

Or suppose I decide to mentor one young man in every year I have left, meeting with each guy for breakfast every other week to coach him on being a loving husband and father. And suppose I influence each of those twenty-eight men to mentor one other man each year of their lives, who in turn would mentor one other man each year. Not too many years pass by before we need a calculator to tabulate the number of husbands, wives, and kids I have influenced for the better. And all this starts at age forty-seven!

In reality, I am working on what I call a "150-year legacy" with regard to all of my children. Let's take our youngest, Kaity, who is presently thirteen, as an example. I am committed to pouring my positive influence into her life and into her children's lives until I die. Let's say that Kaity bears her youngest child at age thirty. Then this grandchild of mine has his or her youngest child—my great-grandchild—at age thirty. And suppose my great-grandchild lives to be eighty-five to a hundred years old.

We are talking about a scenario that stretches out nearly 150 years into the future.

If I do an effective job of investing in the life of my daughter and my grandchild, whom I will know and have opportunity to influence, I expect that my positive investment will trickle down to my great-grandchild, whom I probably won't know—at least not for long. At this rate, my life of influence could be felt for 150 years and beyond. In reality, I hope I am being somewhat conservative on the extent of my influence. It could conceivably last for many generations.

Begin to imagine what can happen when you decide to invest your time and energy in the lives of just a few of the people around you: your spouse, your kids, a coworker, a neighbor. Now imagine encouraging these people to follow your lead and invest themselves in others. I'm talking about becoming a *visionary influencer,* seeing beyond your own life span to generations of influencing people in a positive direction. The operative thought process begins with the words "Imagine what can happen if . . ." I will talk more about this exciting process in part 3 when we look at your passions and dreams, not only what *should* be but what *could* be.

Vectoring in the Finish Phase

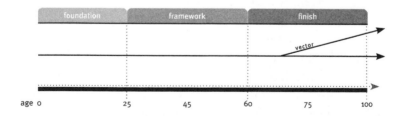

I talk to many people in the finish phase of life who regret that they have squandered a life of influence. They wish they could effect some changes that would make a difference in their world, but they often assume it's already over for them. I try to assure them that it's never too late. In fact, I tell them that they enjoy advantages for influence over most younger people.

Principally, those in the finish phase have experience portfolios bulging with wisdom and knowledge gained from lifelong learning, trial and error, and the college of hard knocks. This wealth of experiences allows them to make more dramatic vector changes that will result in a faster, more dramatic outcome.

For example, you should have more financial resources at this stage, allowing you to direct more money into charitable causes. You have more discretionary hours, allowing you to mentor more people, invest yourself more deeply in your grandchildren, and volunteer your time in the service of others. And you have so much more to share with others because of your great store of experiences and wisdom. You can do a lot in only a little time. The sooner you start, the more you can accomplish and the sooner you will begin to enjoy the satisfaction and fulfillment you have been seeking out of life.

Are you ready to make some vector changes? We'll work on that in the next chapter.

Small Change *Challenges*

- "Every decision you make, every action you take, and every attitude you hold affects the people within your sphere of influence." Determine one vector change you could take in each of the five dimensions of wealth that could have a domino effect.
- Write your plans down and establish a reasonable time frame for completing them.

8

Now What?

---•---

If you agree with the premise that true personal wealth—
the ultimate satisfaction and fulfillment you're seeking in
life—results from investing yourself in others, and if you've
come to see the opportunities ahead by choosing the path
of influence, you're probably wondering, *Now what?*

If you make even a small vector change in your life, you
can turn from the course you're presently traveling and set
your feet on that path of influence. The rest of this book
will help you live out that change.

There are three responses you can make to the lifeWealth
paradigm. Your response may determine if you will ultimately experience true personal wealth. We'll look at these
three options. Then I will tell you why I have chosen a life
of influence and what this path means to me.

Your three choices regarding the lifeWealth paradigm:
reject, ignore, or accept. As you know by now, I believe

this paradigm reflects ultimate truth and will help you experience true personal wealth. But if you are skeptical, let's first explore why you may be tempted to reject or ignore this paradigm.

Reject: "I Don't Buy It"

Those who reject this paradigm are saying in effect, "I have considered the information, but I seriously question or completely deny its validity." They generally come to this conclusion from one of three postures.

Rejecting out of arrogance. This individual states, "I acknowledge the information, but I don't like someone telling me how to live my life. Therefore, I reject your paradigm." The arrogant person sets himself or herself up as judge with little tolerance for direction or instruction outside his or her frame of reference. The danger with this position is that he or she may reject from arrogance something of great value.

Rejecting out of complacency. This individual says, "I acknowledge the information, but I don't really care about its impact on my life or on those around me." This person is satisfied with the status quo. He or she isn't really looking for a change. This person is most likely traveling the default path of indifference.

Rejecting out of self-reliance. This person says, "I acknowledge the information, but I'm quite comfortable with my own viewpoint and conclusion. I'm sure I can achieve true personal wealth on my own." It's difficult to help someone who is content to do it without any help.

Even if you are struggling with the validity of the content at this point, I urge you to continue reading this book. You may change your view about the importance of this information.

124

Ignore: "I Can't Get to It"

This person receives the information and even validates its importance but takes no action. If you are leaning toward ignoring the lifeWealth paradigm, you probably do so for one of three reasons:

Ignoring because of distractions. This person says, "I acknowledge the information, but whenever I try to act on it, something else diverts my attention." Staying the course on the path of influence requires a significant amount of focus and perseverance. If you constantly let other things get in the way, you won't get very far down the road.

Ignoring because of other priorities. This person says, "I acknowledge the information, but as much as I want to act on it, there are so many other pressing issues that require my attention." Everyone must rank his or her priorities in life. Those who do not view a life of influence as a top priority have not grasped the importance of true personal wealth.

Ignoring because of procrastination. This person says, "I acknowledge the information and I intend to act on it. But I just can't find the time right now." This attitude reminds me of a proverb from the Old Testament: "But you, lazybones, how long will you sleep? When will you wake up? I want you to learn this lesson: A little extra sleep, a little more slumber, a little folding of the hands to rest—and poverty will pounce on you like a bandit; scarcity will attack you like an armed robber."[1] Procrastination is the enemy of everything good in life, including the riches of true personal wealth.

If you are tempted to ignore this material for some reason, please keep reading. You may be spurred into action by what you find in part 3.

Act: "I'm Going for It"

This individual receives the information, validates its importance, and takes action. If you see yourself in this category, let me suggest the following steps.

Act by establishing a plan. Part 3 will help you vector toward a life of influence and develop a workable plan for achieving true personal wealth.

Act by assembling a team. The path of influence is not a solo journey. You need others to assist you and encourage you along the way. Throughout the rest of this book, you'll find help on how to assemble a support team, which may include your spouse, an accountability partner, a career counselor, a minister, a financial planner, and others.

Act by taking the first step. Careful planning and good intentions never get anything done. At some point you need to get off the dime and start moving in the direction of your goals. And it begins with the first step. Launching into part 3 is a good way to start.

Act by celebrating your victories. You are embarking on a lifelong journey of becoming a person of influence. You're not perfect, so you will experience both successes and failures. Stay focused on progress, not perfection. And take time to celebrate the victories and progress you make.

Make a Choice

Not too long ago I was in a meeting with a highly successful businessman. Roger's company was on the fast track to success. He was personally earning over half a million dollars a year. But he was putting in sixty to eighty hours a week at the office. He was tired, his marriage was definitely on the path of indifference, and he was missing great experiences with his two young children.

I asked him point-blank, "Roger, are you happy with your life?"

He shook his head. "No, Jerry, I'm not. But the way I figure it, I need to keep up this pace for the next five to ten years. That should get me where I want to be financially and in my career. Then I can become happy and do what I want."

My response was just as direct. "But what will that happiness cost you?"

Roger was going to make a positive vector change . . . someday. But every day he puts off that change he is speeding down a potentially devastating negative path away from his family and a life of influence. He may reach his desired destination of wealth only to learn that he is light-years from the happiness he wants to enjoy.

I encourage you not to delay the action steps I suggested above. The sooner you vector onto the path of influence, the sooner you will begin to experience the joy and fulfillment it has waiting for you.

My Story

We all reach a place in life where we must choose how we will live, what we will live for, and how we will finish life. This decision usually takes place in the foundation or framework phases of life. I believe some key issues help drive this decision. These issues include our ability to understand and come to grips with our past and our disappointments in life, our ability to dream, and most importantly our foundational belief regarding God and the ultimate purpose for living.

While in high school, I made a life-changing decision that has influenced every decision I have made since then. I decided to follow Jesus Christ and his teachings and live a life that is pleasing to him. In effect, that decision started me down the path of influence without me even realizing it. Jesus Christ lived the ultimate life of influence. Though I didn't understand it fully as a teen, my decision to live for Christ was also a decision to live *like* Christ by investing my life in people.

In college I chose to major in urban education, and following graduation I moved to Chicago to live and teach in an inner-city neighborhood. My experiences there contributed to a broader understanding of people and their innate needs regardless of race or socioeconomic status. As a young man I got a good taste of what it means to work hard to contribute to the betterment of others.

Later I returned to my native Iowa, taught in a suburban school, and eventually moved into the business world. Through my journey I continued my quest to live a life that was personally fulfilling by investing my unique abilities in others. As I built my business in the financial services industry, I began to look for ways to impact people more significantly than just advising and assisting them in their pursuit of financial security. I wasn't satisfied with just helping people grow wealthy; I wanted them to experience the fullness of satisfaction and happiness in life.

In 1994 I came across a book that gave me new impetus in my life of influence—*Halftime* by Bob Buford. After reading the book, I determined that my business should become a means to an end, not an end in itself. I wanted to use my skills and experience in my community to help people in the pursuit of true personal wealth.

Over the past fifteen years, I have enjoyed the opportunity and privilege of teaching, motivating, and encouraging people around the country and abroad toward true personal wealth. In addition, I have personally mentored a number of men from different age groups and career paths. These men shared my passion for a life of influence but needed coaching on how to turn that dream into a reality.

I would like to coach you into a fulfilling, satisfying, happy life of influence. If you will allow me to do that, please turn to part 3.

Small Change *Challenges*

- Make a list of all the obstacles that might keep you from following through with your plan for achieving a life of purpose and influence.
- Ask your spouse or a close friend to help you brainstorm solutions and action steps that will help you overcome those obstacles.
- Circle the top three, and commit yourself to a strategy for implementing those vector changes.

Part 3

Strategies
for lifeFocus

9

Focus Your Vision

———————•———————

Glancing ahead between strokes, Florence Chadwick saw nothing but a solid wall of fog. Her body was numb. She had been swimming for nearly sixteen hours. She was already the first woman to swim the English Channel in both directions. Now, at age thirty-four, her goal was to become the first woman to swim the Catalina Channel, twenty-one miles between Catalina Island and the Southern California coast.

On that Fourth of July morning in 1952, the sea was like an ice bath, and the fog was so dense the swimmer could hardly see her support boats. Sharks cruised near her in the water, only to be driven off by rifle shots. Against the frigid grip of the sea, she struggled on—hour after hour—while millions watched on national television.

Alongside Florence in one of the boats, her mother and trainer offered encouragement. They told her it wasn't much farther. But all she could see was fog. They urged her not to quit. She had never quit before. But with only half a mile to go, she asked to be pulled out of the water.

Still thawing her chilled body several hours later, she told a reporter, "Look, I'm not excusing myself. But if I could have seen land I might have made it." It was not fatigue or even the cold that defeated Florence Chadwick that day. It was the fog. Because of the fog, she was unable to see her goal. And without her goal clearly in view, she could not go on.[1]

A wise king said it pointedly: "Where there is no vision, the people perish."[2] You've probably heard a couple of old clichés that phrase it a little differently: "If you aim at nothing, you'll hit it every time"; "If you don't know where you're going, any road will get you there." The vital point, as illustrated by Florence Chadwick's statement to the reporter, is that it's difficult—if not impossible—to accomplish anything of significance if you don't have a crystal-clear vision for where you want to end up and a rock-solid plan for getting you there.

Florence Chadwick didn't give up on conquering the Catalina Channel. Two months later she tried again. This time, despite the dense fog, she swam with her faith intact and her goal firmly anchored in her mind. She knew that somewhere beyond the fog was the California shore, and this time she made it. Florence Chadwick became the first woman to swim the Catalina Channel, eclipsing the men's record by two hours![3]

As you set out on the path of influence to acquire true personal wealth, you need a vision for the journey. Your life vision must be the synthesis of two indispensable elements. The first is your central *purpose* in life. Why are you here? Why do you exist? What do you live for? These are the kinds of questions that will help you determine your life purpose.

We've already discussed the importance of a life of influence. So you may think that's what I'm driving at and answer the big *why* questions by saying, "I exist to live a life of influence."

That's a noble commitment, but I think it falls a little short of describing why you exist. You have a higher purpose than investing your life in others, and I believe that purpose relates to another big *why*. Why would you make such a radical commitment to a life of influence? What moral value, what altruistic motive, what deep truth, what supreme authority leads you to this commitment? Your purpose in life must be rooted in something greater than yourself, something that will outlive you, something that gives ultimate meaning to a life of influence. We will explore this option in the first section of this chapter.

The second indispensable element for your life vision is your *passion*. Whereas your purpose is anchored to something external, your passions erupt from within. What turns your crank? What lights your fire? What moves you emotionally? What touches your soul at the deepest level? These are your passions. There are certain things that you feel especially passionate about. The combination of your passions and your life purpose has a great deal to do with your life vision. In the second section of this chapter we will talk about your passions.

Determine Your Life Purpose

There's a great scene about life purpose in the entertaining comedy *City Slickers*, released in the early 1990s. In the movie, Billy Crystal plays Mitch Robbins, a disillusioned New York City radio ad salesman who is depressed about turning thirty-nine. He is bored with his job, emotionally disconnected from his wife and two kids, and pessimistic about his future.

For his birthday, Mitch's two best friends take him on a big adventure: two weeks of driving cattle from New Mexico to Colorado. It's a riot watching the three city slickers, along with other neophytes on the trail, learn how to ride, rope, and herd cattle. But in the midst of all the adventure, Mitch is still moping about his pointless life.

The trail boss on this cattle drive is a crusty old cowboy named Curly, played by Jack Palance. Curly conscripts a reluctant Mitch to help him round up some strays. Riding alone for a couple of days, the two strike up a conversation, and Mitch confesses his disappointment with his life. Curly says he hears the same thing from other "city folk" on the trail. He says, "You spend about fifty weeks a year getting knots in your rope, and then you think two weeks up here will untie them for you. None of you get it."

Then Curly bores in on Mitch. "Do you know what the secret of life is?"

"No, what?" says Mitch.

Curly raises the index finger on his gloved hand. "This."

Mitch looks puzzled. "Your finger?"

Keeping his finger up, Curly says, "One thing, just one thing. You stick to that and everything else don't mean [bleep]."

"That's great," Mitch responds, sounding a little lost, "but what's the one thing?"

Leveling his finger at Mitch, Curly says, "That's what you've got to figure out."[4]

Curly was talking about a life purpose, one thing you are devoted to above all else. What is your "one thing," the secret of life for you? It may take you a while to "figure out" your one thing. You can devote your life to many things. What will you choose? No one can make that determination except you. And the one thing you decide to center on has a great deal to do with your success at living a life of influence and acquiring true personal wealth.

In the exciting climax to *City Slickers*, Mitch and his two buddies are driving the herd across a river during a storm. A calf flounders in the current and is swept downstream. Mitch, who had delivered the calf on the trail, plunges into the river to rescue it and is caught in the rapids. Mitch's two friends race ahead on the shore and snag him and the calf, saving their lives.

Just before heading home from the airport, the three friends are comparing notes about how their adventure changed them. "I know what this is," Mitch says, raising his finger the way Curly did on the trail. "It's something different for everybody. It's whatever is most important to you. For me, when I was in the river, I was only thinking about one thing. All that other stuff just went away. Only one thing really mattered to me."

At that moment a minivan pulls up to the curb and Mitch's two kids and wife pile out. He embraces them lovingly. Mitch had determined that his family was the most important thing in his life. As the closing credits roll up the screen, Mitch drives his family home to begin living out his purpose.

Your "One Thing"

Author Bob Buford, whose writing has significantly influenced my life, sought out a consultant to help him create a strategic plan for himself. In his book *Halftime*, Buford related how the process began.

Now I needed to draw up a strategic plan for *me*. So I spread out my jumbled dreams and desires, lists of perceived strengths and weaknesses, professions of faith, projects begun and half begun, things to do and things to abandon. It was a quagmire of both complementary and conflicting ambitions, a cacophony of noisy themes and trills of the sort one hears when symphony orchestra musicians are warming up for performance and seeking their pitch.

What should I do? How could I be most useful? Where should I invest my own talents, time, and treasure? What are the values that give purpose to my life? What is the overarching vision that shapes me? Who am I? Where am I? Where am I going? How do I get there?[5]

At this point the consultant asked Buford this question: "What's in the box?" The man explained that there should be one thing "in the box" that was the mainspring of Bob's life. Without that one thing, he would find himself perpetually oscillating between conflicting priorities. Until he was able to identify that one thing, strategic planning was useless. After some serious thinking, Buford concluded that the one thing in the box for him was his commitment to Jesus Christ. It was the "why" of his life. That discovery launched him into the most productive and fulfilling years of his life.

I made this same determination as a high school student, and I have lived out this choice ever since. My relationship with Christ is my "one thing," the overriding purpose for my life. It is the life purpose that God invites all his human creation to adopt. When Christ was asked to identify the greatest commandment, the "one thing" God seeks from us, he quoted from Old Testament law, "'Love the Lord your God with all your heart and with all your soul and with all your mind.' This is the first and greatest commandment."[6]

138

As a Christian, I recognize that my life purpose can be no less than to devote myself to love and serve the God who created me. It is in my relationship with God that I find the direction and motivation for a life of influence, since that is the life Jesus Christ lived. You don't have to choose only one thing to put in the box, leaving everything else behind. That was just the consultant's way of helping Bob Buford focus on what was most important to him. In reality, we walk through life with a number of important things in our box. But you need to land on one thing in your life to guide you and help you relate to all the other important things in your life.

Many people, like Mitch Robbins, decide to live for their spouses and children. That's their "one thing." Such a goal is important; my family is certainly a high priority in my life. But if that's your life purpose, what happens if you lose your spouse, a child, or your entire family in a fatal accident? Does your life suddenly have no meaning? As admirable as it is to devote your life to your family, your ultimate purpose must be based on something more transcendent.

People claim many other noble endeavors as a life purpose. Some have dedicated themselves to serving others, doing what is right, making the world a better place, securing justice for the oppressed, and so on. These are all wonderful priorities, and we admire people who live this way. But why are these traits so admirable? Because they all reflect the character of the God who created us. Sacrificial love, goodness, kindness, righteousness, and justice are the fingerprints of our Maker, and they are all over us.

Whatever you determine to be your life purpose, that choice will significantly impact all dimensions of your experience portfolio. Consider the person who lives for his family. A significant amount of financial capital will likely be directed toward family needs and wants. Things like family vacations and private education for the kids may take priority over such luxuries as buying a new car every year. Family times, such as eating meals together, will have a corner on this person's relational capital. Health, fitness, and recreation may be family rather than solo activities. Investments of intellectual and spiritual capital will similarly be prioritized to benefit family members.

Or think about the person whose top priority in life is to leave the world a better place than she found it. Her life purpose will strongly influence where she spends her discretionary funds, which relationships she gets involved in, and where she invests her abilities. On the earthy side, the indulgent individual, whose chief purpose in life is to "eat, drink, and be merry" for his own pleasure, will direct significant amounts of capital to self-serving ends.

Those who have committed their lives to serving God place their financial, relational, physical, intellectual, and spiritual capital into God's hands to be used as he directs. In fact, you can usually identify someone's chief purpose in life by the way that person disperses lifeWealth capital. Where does a person spend his discretionary money? What kind of people does she hang around with and what kinds of activities is she involved in? In what kind of endeavors does this person invest his skills, education, and experience? All these investments of capital will point to the thing that is most important to this person, whether or not she has consciously determined this is what is most important to her.

Sharpening Focus in Tough Times

Life purpose seems to come into sharper focus during times of crisis. Tragedy, pain, loss, and great stress motivate us to reevaluate what is most important to us. Mitch said that he discovered his "one thing" as he tumbled down the rapids, fearing he might drown.

During harrowing experiences we are ready to jettison a lot of stuff that suddenly doesn't count for much in order to latch on to what really does matter to us. That's the hidden blessing of tough times: They often help us identify or renew our dedication to our life purpose.

Countless Americans received a wake-up call on September 11, 2001. One such individual was a man I met recently. Tom worked on an upper floor of one of the World Trade Center buildings.

On the morning of September 11, 2001, Tom went into work a little later than usual because of a late meeting the night before. As he neared the World Trade Center, he watched in horror as the building in which he had worked collapsed, killing thousands. The death toll from his company was over sixty. Had Tom arrived at the office at his regular time, he would likely have been one of them.

As the reality of this terrible event began to sink in, Tom recalled that he had connected to and provided the kind of leadership and encouragement that he desired with only a handful of his colleagues who had perished. He realized how many opportunities had come and gone, hearing himself always say, "There will be another time."

On September 12, 2001, Tom had the same purpose in life he had on September 10. But because of the tragic events of 9-11, his purpose was, and has remained, in sharper focus. Tom has a new urgency for being the kind of leader God called him to be, sharing the hope of his faith with others and investing himself unselfishly in those with whom he has daily contact. I talked with Tom recently, and he related to me what has happened since his wake-up call. As he has more intently led his organization and shared his hope and passion for life, others have discovered a renewed sense of purpose and made vector changes in their own lives. The compounding effect of Tom's vector change is far-reaching, and it will likely influence countless others in ways he will never know about.

Discovering Your Passions

A life purpose needs to be greater than we are, something that will outlive us. A life purpose meeting these criteria can be huge, and the task of living out that purpose daunting. Consider some of the more common purposes. Here is someone who has chosen to devote his life to making the world a better place. What a massive mission! World population is nearing six billion people. How does this person know where to start? How can he hope to make a dent in his lifetime?

Or here's another person committed to fighting for justice for the downtrodden and oppressed. There are more victims in our country alone than can be helped in three lifetimes. Where will she focus? Which causes of justice will she champion? Which oppressed persons will receive her aid?

Even a person like Mitch Robbins, who decides to live for his family, is taking on a giant-sized task. There's no way he can be involved and influential in every corner of each family member's life. It would be a full-time job and then some.

As a Christian, my life purpose is also enormous. I have committed my life to glorify God and do his will. This is a global mission enveloping all dimensions of lifeWealth and stretching beyond time into eternity. How can I get my arms around such a purpose to the point that anything is accomplished?

I believe the answer to the dilemma of a bigger-than-life purpose is found in discovering your passions. In order to bring your life vision into clear focus, you need to hear what your heart is telling you to do, not just where your head is telling you to go. Your passions will help you discover exactly where you are suited and motivated to live out your purpose.

Think of your purpose and passions as the crosshairs in a rifle scope. Your purpose is like the horizontal line in the scope. Your passions can be compared to the vertical line in the scope. If you have one line without the other, you're not sure where to aim. The two intersecting lines are necessary to help you hit your target. Purpose alone can take you all over the map. But when you bring your passions into play, you can draw a bead on a manageable vision for your life.

For example, let's go back to the person who has sold out to make the world a better place. It's an admirable goal, but without a clear vision for accomplishing it, can anything get done? So let's ask this person, "What part of the hurting world most deeply touches you? What area appeals to both your concern and your ability to effect a change?"

I can imagine a number of answers: "I'm very concerned about world hunger, and I would enjoy volunteering for an agency like the Red Cross." "I believe abortion is wrong, and I might want to run for public office in my community to help voice the concerns of others like me." "The death and destruction caused by gang activity in my community breaks my heart. I relate well to kids. Maybe I should volunteer to be a mentor."

Do you see how discovering your deep passions can help bring your purpose and vision into focus? Your passions narrow down the expanse of your overall purpose to a smaller "target," something you can handle. Discovering your passions will also provide needed impetus for your actions. We all do our best and most significant work when our hearts are in it, when we are passionate about what we are doing. Conversely, even the noblest tasks become drudgery when we lack the inner fire to keep us going.

Passions will also help direct our investment of life-Wealth capital. The person whose purpose is to improve the world and whose passion is to relieve world hunger has narrowed the field for investing his life. Instead of spreading his charitable donations across twenty relief agencies, perhaps he focuses the majority of his giving on the Red Cross and a few other organizations majoring on hunger relief. He will likely seek out other people to influence toward his mission. He will offer his unique abilities in service of the Red Cross. If he is experienced in sales, perhaps he will volunteer to solicit donations from businesses in the community. Once purpose and passion merge to create vision, you have a tangible, realistic target for investing your life.

I have three consuming passions. As a Christian, my purpose is to serve Christ wholeheartedly and live a life of influence for him. In reality, my purpose stretches to every corner of who I am and what I do. But my real vision for my life came into focus when I identified my passions in light of my purpose to serve Christ. The following three passions give my purpose clear direction:

1. I am passionate about building a marriage relationship with Nancy that mirrors God's love for his people.
2. I am passionate about raising our kids to reverence God and serve Jesus Christ.

144

3. I am passionate about using my unique gifts, abilities, and experiences to encourage others toward living a life of influence.

This lifeFocus is at the center of all my lifeWealth capital investments outside of caring for my family. I have spent a lot of my own money developing the material I present in conferences and seminars and in this book. Much of my relational capital is invested in the many groups of people around the country to whom I present this material. I have purposely turned over to others the day-to-day operation of my company in order to invest my skills and expertise in sharing this message. The more my purpose and passions come together to form a clear vision for my life, the more fulfilled and satisfied I feel. It's a taste of true personal wealth I want to share with everyone I meet. The icing on the cake is hearing others say they are experiencing true personal wealth as a result of what I have shared with them. For me, life doesn't get any better than that!

So what are your passions? If they seem a little fuzzy to you, do a life reflection exercise. Imagine yourself as a ninety-year-old gazing back over your life. Which experiences and memories would bring you the most joy and satisfaction? It's likely that those anticipated highlights will indicate areas of your passion.

For example, Kent, a friend and colleague of mine, says that thirty years from now he wants to be sitting around the table with his children and grandchildren, reflecting on their life together as a family and laughing. In other words, he dreams of growing older as the patriarch of a family that gets along well and enjoys being together. In light of Kent's reflection, I'd say he is passionate about building harmony and fun into his family.

Whatever you do especially well and enjoy doing is likely an area of your personal passion that, when intersected with your purpose, will help focus the vision for your life. Do you have artistic talent and love to paint or decorate? Are you mechanically inclined, able to build or fix just about anything? Are you a topflight people person, able to shine in social settings? Are you especially good at organizing and administering details? Look for ways you can use your passion and ability to accomplish your chosen purpose. And if you are unsure where your unique abilities and passions lie, we will share some guidelines in chapter 10 to help you identify these areas.

Small Change *Challenges*

- Summarize in one or two sentences your "one thing" in the box. (This is your purpose.)
- Write another paragraph describing the things you are passionate about.
- With a clearer understanding of your purpose and passion, identify one vector change that you need to make in your life that will sharpen your focus and create a greater sense of alignment.

10

Live Purposefully

———•———

All successful corporations and organizations have visionaries at the top. These people are often criticized for living with their heads in the clouds. More realistically, however, visionaries usually soar above the clouds. They have a knack for seeing the big picture. They can look beyond a problem to imagine grand and profitable solutions. The needs of others can trigger dozens of creative ideas for meeting those needs faster, more efficiently, and more economically. Visionaries live outside the box.

You're sitting in a meeting at ABC Enterprises. The sales manager says, "Our competitor, XYZ Industries, has just come up with a superwidget that outperforms our widget at the same retail price. We can't compete with XYZ." All eyes turn to the head of the table.

Company president Jones leans back in his chair, gazing out the window. He looks as if he is thinking about vacation on a Caribbean island. After several silent moments he leans forward. "All right, here's what we do. We come up with a new widget that matches XYZ's for performance. But we'll equip ours with double capacity, increase the speed 20 percent, and offer it in four designer colors. We kick up the price but hammer the market with its value and versatility." Mr. Jones then smiles and shrugs a no-brainer shrug. "Now, shall we call out for kung pao chicken and lo mein?"

That's a visionary. Problem stated; problem solved; let's do lunch. But most of the ABC team will skip lunch today. They all agree that a new widget is the way to go. But Mr. Jones's excellent vision, stated in three sweeping sentences, has just created a ton of work for everyone else. Research and development, manufacturing, marketing and sales, and shipping all have to retool for this big move. Personnel must hire more people. Building supervision needs to find more space. The ripple effect of the president's vision will impact everyone in his organization for months to come.

I have oversimplified the scenario, of course. But my point is that a vision, whether it is for a corporation or for your life, must be followed by purposeful action or the vision is worthless. ABC Enterprises would go bankrupt if Mr. Jones didn't have a team of skilled individuals to implement his vision for the company's productivity, growth, and success. That's the way it is with many visionaries. Their thing is the big picture, the vision and excitement of what can happen. But they are not always as skilled or interested in making the vision happen. Visionaries need organizers, administrators, and a myriad of nuts-and-bolts people to make the vision a reality.

There's a big difference between a corporate vision and your vision for a life of influence leading to true personal wealth. Mr. Jones at ABC has a skilled team to implement his vision; you are basically on your own to implement

148

your vision. Once you focus your vision at the intersection of your overall purpose and your unique passions, you can't pass it off to someone else who will make it happen. Sure, you will take advantage of the coaching and counsel of others from time to time. And you are wise to diligently seek God's wisdom and guidance for your life. But the ultimate responsibility for living out your vision by making timely vector changes rests on your shoulders. If you don't pursue your purpose and passions with a plan of action, your vision will die from neglect.

How do you move strategically in the direction of your vision? It's largely a matter of intentionality—living your life on purpose. Purposeful living means that you have a reason for why you do what you do and don't do what you don't do. You choose to do those things that help you become the person you want to be, and you choose to avoid other things because they do *not* help you become the person you want to be.

Three significant elements enable you to live out your vision intentionally and purposefully. First, as I mentioned in the previous chapter, you need to identify your unique abilities and implement them in living out your vision. Second, you need to grab your life by the horns and live proactively instead of reactively. Third, you need to participate in the ongoing, cyclical process of assessing where you are, strategizing where you want to be, taking action on that strategy, and evaluating your progress. In this chapter we will consider these three vital elements.

Zero In on Your Unique Abilities

Allow me to sketch a couple of scenes for you.

At a busy downtown intersection, a careless driver runs a red light and crashes into a car that had the right of way.

In the seconds following the accident, several witnesses respond:

- One person immediately rushes to each car to see if anyone is injured.
- Another person whips out a cell phone and dials 911.
- Someone else jumps into the street to direct traffic around the tangled autos.
- One person rushes up to the car of the driver at fault and starts bawling him out for his carelessness.
- Another individual stands on the sidewalk silently calculating the amount of damage each car suffered.
- Someone else takes charge, barking instructions to other onlookers about what to do.
- Yet another person starts taking down names and phone numbers of witnesses to give to the victim.
- One individual backs away from the bustling scene, not wanting to be involved.

Put yourself in that intersection. Which of the people above do you think most closely mirrors your response in the situation?

There is a big party going on in a crowded home. The many people in attendance are involved in a number of ways:

- One partygoer is the consummate social butterfly, flitting around, talking to everyone personally.
- Then there's the life-of-the-party type who is loud, telling jokes, laughing with everyone, entertaining the crowd at large.

- Another person at the party just wants to be useful, volunteering to replenish the hors d'oeuvres, toting used glasses to the kitchen, etc.
- One person sits quietly in the corner watching the others, speaking cordially but only when spoken to.
- Another person is positioned near the TV in a corner of the family room, more interested in the program than in the party.
- Someone else monitors the CD player, making sure appropriate background music is playing.

Suppose you had been invited to this party. Which of these people most closely represents the role you would play?

Exercises like these remind us that everyone is unique. We have an assortment of talents, skills, and traits. Our upbringing and education have further shaped who we are and how we respond to the world around us. So witnesses to the same accident respond differently based on how they are wired. People party differently in response to their unique mix of personality and ability. It's the same in any area of human activity and relationship. We all come into the framework phase of our lives as different from anyone else in appearance and ability as we are in DNA.

Among your array of gifts, abilities, and talents are at least a couple that really shine. These are the areas in which you are better than average and from which you gain much personal satisfaction. These areas may include music, art, writing, speaking, mechanics, athletics, intelligence, intuition, organization, administration, math/science, language, and many more. You may be a winsome people person. You may be a deep-thinking problem solver. Perhaps you are a natural-born leader or

151

a meticulous detail person. Whatever it is, your bundle of abilities helps make you unique.

Yet I am amazed at the number of people I talk to who have never clearly identified or maximized their unique abilities. These are the areas in which you are predisposed to the greatest success. These are the areas in which you can usually accomplish the most, effect the greatest good, and be most fully energized and fulfilled in the process. Yet how many of us are really making the most of our primary abilities?

Too often we get drawn into activities and roles that do not utilize our unique abilities. Often those activities require skills and abilities that are clearly not among our strengths, diverting precious time and energy from our strengths. And these weaker elements usually tax our time heavily, because they don't come naturally for us.

A good goal for achieving the best efficiency is to work toward spending 60–80 percent of our time doing the things for which we are most gifted and limiting our lesser skills to 20–40 percent. Unfortunately, the opposite is often true for most people.

Beyond my commitment to family, my vision is for teaching and encouraging others in the pursuit of true personal wealth. My purpose and passion are specifically focused on speaking and writing to people about how they can find enriching satisfaction and fulfillment in a life of influence.

I have boundless energy for this vision. My happiest days are the ones during which I get to teach these principles. So I am methodically delegating other responsibilities in order to invest myself more fully to living out my vision. And I encourage you to do the same.

A word of caution here: I am *not* saying that you should bail out of all activities that don't fully utilize your unique abilities. We all have tasks and responsibilities that must be accomplished whether we are gifted for them or not. Even if you are not a people person, you have to deal with people. You can seek a job that is more task-centered than people-centered, but you can't wall yourself off just because you're not gifted in social skills.

Furthermore, I don't recommend that you quit an entry-level job just because the position taps into few of your abilities. You need a job, and sometimes you must take work where you can find it. However, there is no harm in applying for more suitable positions inside or outside the company that move you closer to the kind of work you really want to do. Over the course of your employment, you should be constantly moving toward the center of your best, most fulfilling skills.

Even when you are not in the center of your unique abilities, you are making valuable deposits in your experience portfolio. Even these lesser tasks help you build equity, moving you closer to living out your purpose. Before launching into my career as a financial planner, I taught eighth grade in the inner city of Chicago and fifth grade in the suburbs of Des Moines. I also worked in sales. While these positions did not utilize my greatest strengths, each experience made a valuable contribution to my overall development.

The objective is to be continually moving toward majoring in the areas of your ability and minoring in the areas in which you are not as skilled. It's a lifetime process. But with every step toward that goal, you will sense greater satisfaction and impetus to keep moving.

Discovering Your Sweet Spot

How do you identify the areas of your unique ability? You probably have some idea what they are already, and you may also be aware of the areas that are definitely not your strengths. But how do you know for sure?

There are many professionally designed instruments to help you identify such qualities as personality traits, shades of temperament, work skills, and spiritual gifts. Some of these exercises are administered and interpreted by counselors who are trained to help you identify your unique abilities. Others you can do yourself, and the self-help section at the local bookstore is full of these kinds of tools.

In the meantime, here is a simple exercise that will get you thinking. It's a series of questions designed to lead you from your personal experiences and accomplishments to the skills and abilities behind them.

Think of a recent time when you found yourself involved in something with tireless enthusiasm. It was so enjoyable and fulfilling you had a hard time pulling yourself away from it. Or you were so engrossed that time seemed to fly by. When that activity concluded, you looked forward to doing it again.

You may be thinking of a particular task you do at your place of employment, such as talking to customers on the phone, running a training meeting, designing a better system, helping people find what they need, organizing a supply room, or balancing the books. It's a task for which you might be tempted to say, "If I could just do this all the time, I'd work for free."

You may be thinking of an activity you are involved in strictly as a volunteer, such as visiting patients at the hospital, being a mentor to students, raising funds for a worthy cause, teaching a Sunday school class, coaching a kids' soccer team, or serving meals at a rescue mission. This activity prompts you to consider, "If I could get paid for doing this, I'd quit my job in a heartbeat."

Perhaps a household activity comes to mind. You love the satisfaction of redecorating a room, designing and maintaining a backyard garden, building an addition to the house, or reorganizing the garage. Or you may be thinking about a leisure activity: backpacking, stargazing, playing racquetball, restoring an antique car, reading about history, wrestling on the floor with your grandchildren, or taking and developing photographs. I'm talking about anything you do that you can't seem to get enough of.

Another way to discover this area of skill and interest is to talk to the people who know you well: parents, spouse, children, close friends, minister. Ask them: "From your observation, where do you think I excel? What are my best qualities? Where do you see me having the greatest personal success and fulfillment?" Interview at least ten people and you will begin to notice similarities in their responses and to discover the unique abilities that run like a thread through all areas of your life.

You probably have something in mind by now, so let's start there. Think carefully through the following questions as they relate to the activity that brings you so much satisfaction. They should give you a strong clue about your unique ability:

1. What specific skills were you using in this activity?
2. Why was this activity appealing to you?
3. Why did this activity seem important or valuable to you?
4. Why did this activity energize you?
5. Why do you want to go back to this activity?

As I worked through this questioning process with my activities, I kept coming up with the same answers. It became clear to me that my unique ability is motivating people. I seem to be gifted at encouraging and empowering others to stretch beyond their comfort zone and become the best

155

they can possibly be. Speaking energizes me. I love to see people identify their giftedness, set goals for themselves, and establish a plan for achieving those goals. I love to motivate and assist people toward making good choices across all the dimensions of lifeWealth. This is the center of the highway on the life of influence for me. This is my sweet spot, and I'm having the time of my life.

I encourage you to continue on this journey toward discovering your unique abilities. The more you know about yourself, your strengths, your gifts, and your talents, the better prepared you are for fulfilling your life vision—and having a great time doing it!

Start Living Proactively

You don't have to know everything about your life vision, your purpose and passion, and your unique abilities before you can begin making significant strides down the path of influence. You can start moving now based on what you already know. The experience of the journey will teach you volumes about yourself. Every experience, both good and bad, equips you for a more focused journey. As Samuel Butler said, "Don't learn to do, but learn in doing. Let your falls not be on a prepared ground, but let them be *bona fide* falls in the rough and tumble of the world."[1]

Yet in order to make the most of our experiences and what they teach us, we need to understand the difference between living reactively and living proactively. Our natural tendency is to react to life as it happens instead of taking an active role in where we are headed and what we will accomplish. Rita Mae Brown said, "A life of reaction is a life of slavery, intellectually and spiritually. One must fight for a life of action, not reaction."[2]

Reactive living is a clear indicator that we are out of touch with our life vision. We are meandering down the path of life instead of purposely striding toward a predetermined destination. Our life experiences determine our direction instead of our direction helping us respond to our life experiences. We assess what will happen in the future based on what has happened to us in the past. We are hindered from moving forward into new experiences by seven deadly words: "I've never done it this way before."

Notice the difference between reactive living and proactive living as it might look in each of the five dimensions of lifeWealth.

Financial capital. Reactive living bases spending on the money that comes in and the bills in the drawer. Proactive living controls spending on the basis of a budget.

Relational capital. In reactive living, your relationships are formed from the people you encounter in the course of life. In proactive living, you also initiate and nurture relationships based on your life vision.

Physical capital. Reactive people don't take control until the doctor says, "You're working too hard," or "You're thirty pounds overweight." Proactive people monitor their own health and fitness, or are at least consistent about wellness checkups.

Intellectual capital. Reactive people sign up for the program that is most desperate for volunteer help instead of looking for the program that best utilizes their unique abilities. Proactive people are continually looking for ways to learn new skills and improve their performance in their areas of strength and look for ways to advance their career and pursue new opportunities.

Spiritual capital. Reactive people don't give God much thought until something goes wrong or they're in trouble and need divine help. Proactive people seek to know God and explore his claim on their lives.

Reactive living causes a person to wait for opportunities instead of create or initiate opportunities. Reactive living prompts a victim's mind-set. As they are buffeted by life experiences, these people say things like, "Life is not fair," or "Things never go my way." They take a defensive posture in life, spending their energy evading pain, hurt, and uncertainty instead of charging ahead while dealing with the inevitable pain, hurt, and uncertainty that attend any worthwhile endeavor.

Proactive living is creating a strategy for mapping out a course in all dimensions of life and moving ahead with that course. It's the process of making a plan and working the plan in your life based on your vision. You might be able to catch the flavor of proactive living in the following passage from the Old Testament. The formerly exiled nation of Israel stands at the border of the land God has commanded them to fight for and occupy. As the nation awaits the command to go, God gives Joshua, Israel's leader, this challenge:

> Be strong and courageous, because you will lead these people to inherit the land I swore to their forefathers to give them. Be strong and very courageous. Be careful to obey all the law my servant Moses gave you; do not turn from it to the right or to the left, that you may be successful wherever you go. Do not let this Book of the Law depart from your mouth; meditate on it day and night, so that you may be careful to do everything written in it. Then you will be prosperous and successful. Have I not commanded you? Be strong and courageous. Do not be terrified; do not be discouraged, for the Lord your God will be with you wherever you go.[3]

Can you hear the "take charge" attitude in these words? The nation's prosperity and success were directly linked to Joshua and the people moving forward courageously and

158

obeying God's commands carefully, without deviating. It was not enough to know what to do; they were being called to get their act together, move out with strength and courage, and do the job. It was a call to proactive living.

If you are going to fulfill your life vision and experience true personal wealth, you must proactively take control of what you do and where you're going. And instead of reacting to circumstances you cannot plan or control, you must choose to live responsively by integrating those life experiences into your plans and objectives.

Continually Work the Process

Living proactively is not a one-time decision. It is a process that assures you will stay on course with your life vision. I call it the lifeFocus process. The four elements of the process are easy to remember by the acronym ASAP: assessment, strategy, action, progress. As the graphic illustrates, the lifeFocus process is cyclical—it just keeps rolling along. As you continue to assess, strategize, act, and note progress, you will find yourself moving steadily down the road toward your vision. Let's look at each phase of the process.

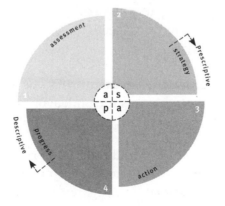

Assessment

Periodically you need to look at where you are in light of where you want to be. Don't expend too much time or energy on the journey without making sure you are on course. Frequent assessment will minimize unprofitable rabbit trails away from your vision. Let's consider an example.

Andrea, a working mother, has a vision for mentoring younger women who want to blend family and career. She has allotted time in her schedule to meet once a month with two women for a period of six months. Her goal is to lead them through a series of key questions and exercises to help them balance these two significant roles in their lives.

Andrea's initial assessment may take the form of some questions like these:

1. Have I identified at least two working women I want to contact about my availability to mentor?
2. Will I contact them via e-mail, letter, or personal phone call?
3. Have I prepared the questions and exercises I want to use?
4. Will I give them "homework" between sessions? Shall I create worksheets for our sessions and homework?

Once she is involved in mentoring one or two women, she can and should assess the endeavor while in process. Questions like these might be helpful to her:

1. Are the questions and exercises provoking helpful, productive interaction with these women? How do I know?

2. Is one meeting a month sufficient for this process?
3. Are the women bringing up good topics I had not anticipated but need to accommodate?
4. Have I identified at least two more women for the next six-month session?

No matter what your individual vision may be, the basic assessment issue on the path of influence is "Am I indeed providing a positive influence? If so, what is causing it to happen? If not, why not?"

Strategy

Once you have an idea where you are on the journey, chart a course to your destination. This is your strategy for realizing your vision. And as you periodically assess your progress, you have the opportunity to tweak that strategy.

Here are several items Andrea might consider as she plots her course to mentor young working mothers.

1. Contact Elise, Kim, Megan, and Georgette by phone to see if they are interested in being mentored. If more than two are interested, see if they are willing to wait six months till the next session.
2. Write questions and exercises and ask Chuck to evaluate them, since he has been mentoring guys at his church. Implement any helpful suggestions.
3. Block out my monthly calendar for the days I will meet with the first two women.
4. Write and photocopy final materials.

As Andrea meets with the first two women, she may tweak her strategy. She may decide that she could mentor three women during the next six-month session. She may realize that she has overestimated what the women can accomplish and decide to scale back the questions and exercises to a more manageable number. And at midpoint during the first session, she will need to strategize how to approach the second group of women.

Strategies should never be cast in cement. They will change and improve as you progress through the journey.

Action

You can assess and strategize all you want, but until you act on your plan, you will be no closer to realizing your vision. It's like the captain of the ship setting a course but never leaving the harbor. He can set the course and even change coordinates, but if he hasn't set sail, he has done nothing more than point his ship in a particular direction or turn and face another direction. Without forward movement, the ship will stay in the same spot. If you have effectively assessed your situation and created a clear strategy, it is time to start working your plan. You will have plenty of opportunities along the way to fine-tune your assessment and strategy along the way. That's what vectors are all about.

Feeling nervous and a little unsure, Andrea begins the first six-month mentoring session with Kim and Megan. She diligently keeps in contact with them throughout each month, not just through their scheduled meetings but by e-mail and phone. Andrea invites the women to call her if they have questions about the exercises. These conversations blossom into some wonderful teachable moments. It's a fruitful part of mentoring she had not anticipated.

By the third month, Andrea also realizes that her commitment to Kim and Megan is taking more time than she planned. But she is so energized by how the women are responding that she cannot back down. With encouragement from her husband, Andrea cuts back her time commitment in a couple of other areas. She can envision a time when she can scale back her own work to devote more time to women who are struggling with home and career pressures. Putting her strategy into action has further heightened Andrea's passion for encouraging young women.

The action stage of the process should be as rewarding and fulfilling for you as it was for Andrea. After all, you should be operating in your areas of greatest strength and satisfaction. You may still struggle in some areas, but that's to be expected. Even when pursuing your vision, you will encounter roadblocks and hurdles along the way. But you can continually go back to the drawing board in the assessment and strategy stages of your lifeWealth process to work through these difficulties.

Progress

Andrea had mixed feelings at the end of the first six-month session. She was excited about Kim and Megan's responses to the exercises. She felt they had made some significant strides in achieving better balance between their role as wives and mothers and their careers. But she was disappointed because the two women had not completely fulfilled her expectations for them. At times, near the end of the session, Andrea felt she had failed them. She experienced moments of uncertainty, wondering if she had missed her vision.

Living out your vision is a lifelong process. You may have an ideal for where you want to be at some point in your life. Unfortunately, ideals are rarely attainable. So

163

instead of measuring your efforts against the phantom of perfection, learn to enjoy what progress you make. Remember: If you continually measure yourself by how far you have yet to go, you will be disappointed. But if you turn around and see how far you have come, you will see progress.

Andrea decided to focus on the progress she had made with Kim and Megan instead of moping over what she had not accomplished. She realized that her relationship with the women would continue, though at a lower level of involvement. In the meantime, she moved energetically into retooling the exercises for Darla and Wendy, who would be starting with her in a few weeks. She anticipated even greater progress with these two women.

As you continually assess, strategize, and act, don't forget to check for progress. Note your accomplishments. Celebrate the victories and learn from the setbacks. Make a conscious effort to deposit the wisdom, knowledge, and insights you gain from both into your experience portfolio in order to increase your equity. And where there is room for improvement, take any steps necessary as you continue to cycle through the assessment, strategy, and action stages.

As you proactively move down the path toward your vision, you should continually develop and improve your methods of influence. There are a number of ways you can sharpen yourself for greater success. In chapter 11 we will explore several of these methods.

Small Change *Challenges*

- What do you think are your unique abilities?

- "Proactive living is creating a strategy for mapping out a course in all dimensions of life and moving ahead with that course." What are three vector changes that you could initiate today that could facilitate the use of your unique abilities more effectively?

11

Equip for Success

———————●———————

One of the many parables Jesus told introduces another
strategy for acquiring true personal wealth. Jesus told
these stories to illustrate principles for relating to God
and his activity in the world. The scene of this parable is
the preparation for a Jewish wedding. Jesus says,

> The Kingdom of Heaven can be illustrated by the story of
> ten bridesmaids who took their lamps and went to meet
> the bridegroom. Five of them were foolish, and five were
> wise. The five who were foolish took no oil for their lamps,
> but the other five were wise enough to take along extra oil.
> When the bridegroom was delayed, they all lay down and
> slept. At midnight they were roused by the shout, "Look,
> the bridegroom is coming! Come out and welcome him!"
> All the bridesmaids got up and prepared their lamps.
> Then the five foolish ones asked the others, "Please give
> us some of your oil because our lamps are going out." But

the others replied, "We don't have enough for all of us. Go to a shop and buy some for yourselves."

But while they were gone to buy oil, the bridegroom came, and those who were ready went in with him to the marriage feast, and the door was locked. Later, when the other five bridesmaids returned, they stood outside, calling, "Sir, open the door for us!" But he called back, "I don't know you!"

So stay awake and be prepared, because you do not know the day or hour of my return.[1]

One of the mistakes many people make with Jesus' parables is to read too much into them. They are distracted by the details of the story. They wonder, "What does the oil represent? Why did Jesus talk about ten bridesmaids instead of six or two? What did the bridegroom mean when he said, 'I don't know you'?" In reality, Jesus' intent in each story was to illustrate one simple principle. And he often summarized his parables by stating clearly what he was driving at.

Concluding the parable of the ten bridesmaids, Jesus admonished, "Stay awake and be prepared." Jesus called the five bridesmaids who did stay awake and prepared wise; the five who didn't he called foolish. Jesus says to us, "Don't get lazy and squander your opportunities for living out your vision. Rather, stay alert and be prepared to make the most of every opportunity, because you don't know how much time you have left."

When it comes to living a life of influence in harmony with your vision, you are wise to do everything you can to equip yourself for success, and you are foolish to drift along ill-prepared for your mission. It's all about being a wise steward of the abilities, purpose, and passion God has given you. It's about being the best you can be at what you feel called to do in the lives of others.

What would you think about a physician who stops learning, researching, and sharpening his skills once he leaves medical school? His attitude is "Hey, I paid good money for my education. I'll just practice what I learned to the best of my ability. Who needs more?" He sure wouldn't be my doctor. I want a doctor who is up-to-date on the latest diseases, procedures, and medicines; who attends conferences, reads the latest medical journals, and upgrades his practice by implementing what he learns. Why? Because he has maximized his prospect of correctly diagnosing and successfully treating my physical problems. He is better equipped to succeed.

Your life vision may not involve saving lives, but your calling to influence those around you is no less important. You have integrated your purpose and passions with your unique abilities, and a life vision has come into focus. You have set a course and begun to navigate in the direction of the true personal wealth that results from living out that vision. But you are not yet fully equipped for all the experiences you will face. In fact, you will always need to further sharpen your abilities and deepen your passion.

To be the best you can be as you journey the path of influence, you must equip yourself continually for success. I see four specific ways this can be accomplished. First, always keep learning about yourself, your abilities, and your particular areas of expertise and service to others. Second, continually tap into your experience portfolio to help you interpret and resolve new experiences. Third, enlist and rely upon a team of helpful and supportive individuals. Fourth, work to balance how you allocate your time in relation to your priorities. Let's consider these four strategies for being a wise steward of your abilities and passions.

169

Become a Lifelong Learner

An excellent way to make the most of your opportunities to influence others is to learn all you can about what you are doing in order to continually improve at it. I'm not talking about grandiose or mysterious activities here, but about everyday stuff anyone can do. Simply apply these skills to your area of passion and activity. Here are some examples:

- Read books, magazines, journals, and trade publications.
- Research topics and join news groups on the Internet.
- Enroll in classes, seminars, conferences, and workshops.
- Interview experts in your field of interest.
- Seek insights and advice from others who do what you're doing.
- Ask your friends to be on the lookout for material and resources you might be able to use.
- Keep a card file, notebook, or data file on the computer to help you easily access information you have collected in the past.

Part of my ongoing learning takes place at the local bookstore. I spend half a day perusing books and taking notes. You can do the same kind of thing in the public library. I browse through the self-help section for new resources on the topics of life purpose, influence, personal enrichment, and so on. Often I find salient information and quotes to help me fine-tune my talks at conferences and hone my mentoring curriculum. And I buy my share of books, so I'm not just taking up space.

170

Your approach to learning in your area of investment in others will be unique to your personality, learning style, and available time. No two people are alike, so no two people learn the same way. The point is to resist the temptation to settle for the status quo and discipline yourself to be an ongoing learner. It will enrich your life and equip you for success as you influence others.

In his book *How to Think Like Leonardo da Vinci*, Michael Gelb gives insight into the person many people believe to be the most intelligent ever to live. "Leonardo knew the importance of continuous learning. 'Just as iron rusts from disuse, and stagnant water putrefies, or when cold turns to ice, so our intellect wastes unless it is kept in use.' The continuous quest for learning is the powerhouse of the da Vincian spirit."[2]

Tap Into Your Experience Portfolio

The dramatic film *The Last Castle* is about a fictional U.S. military prison located in a fortresslike complex that was once a castle. The prisoners are soldiers who have committed a wide variety of crimes, and the warden is a bitter army colonel who has never commanded troops in battle. He and the guards treat the inmates cruelly, as if they were prisoners of war.

One day, recently court-martialed General Eugene Irwin, played by Robert Redford, arrives at the prison. A decorated and respected military leader, Irwin had made a mistake in battle, sending his men into a situation against the direct orders of the president of the United States. Lives were lost, and Irwin was sentenced to ten years in the castle. He settles in to do his time and go home without getting involved in prison politics.

171

But the cruel and inhumane treatment of the prisoners and the warden's personal vendetta against him motivates Irwin to change his mind. Having been a POW in Vietnam, Irwin passes along tips for surviving the cruelties of life in the castle. An experienced leader, he quietly wins the confidence of the other prisoners. Irwin covertly organizes the men into a disciplined military unit. Under the general's leadership, the prisoners lead a revolt and succeed in getting the maniacal warden dismissed.

General Irwin's battle-proven leadership experience made all the difference. Before he came along, the prisoners languished in hopelessness. By applying his experience to the situation, Irwin restored unity, esprit de corps, and direction among the prisoners, and a great wrong was defeated. The general's vast experience, and his willingness to apply it to the situation at hand, allowed him to wield a positive influence in the lives of scores of men.

Your experience portfolio is one of your most valuable resources for a life of influence. All life experiences, positive and negative, can be useful in helping others navigate through their challenges and difficulties. Our past successes and failures contribute to our internal database for processing future experiences and making decisions. Each succeeding experience adds to that database.

Your successes increase your confidence. Each success is like a single brick in a wall. As you add bricks to the wall with each new victory, it becomes more formidable in size and strength. Patriot Patrick Henry said, "I have but one lamp by which my feet are guided; and that is the lamp of experience. I know of no way of judging the future but by the past."[3]

Even your failures can raise your confidence level. Every time you survive a failure, you gain confidence to try again, and your fear of failure diminishes. On the positive side, your failures become the testing ground for what works and doesn't work. Henry Ford wisely stated, "Failure is only the opportunity to begin again more intelligently."[4] These experiences may help you decide which activities you should delegate to others or eliminate from your life altogether.

This is an excellent time for introspection. Ask yourself, "Why did I fail? What should I have done differently? How could I do it more successfully?"

Make the most of all your life experiences. Learn from them and file them away for future reference. Draw from this wealth as you invest your life in others.

Enlist a Support Team

You can do one thing in life to virtually guarantee your failure: Try to make it on your own. King Solomon wrote, "As iron sharpens iron, a friend sharpens a friend."[5] He pictures a metal tool or weapon that has become dull and worn with use. The only way that implement will remain useful and effective is when it is regularly sharpened on another piece of metal just as hard or harder. Similarly, if you are not continually sharpened by people who care for you and are committed to your success, you will become as useless as a dull knife.

There are two areas in which we all need skilled, knowledgeable, helpful people on our side. These two areas certainly overlap, but I want to talk about them separately. One is the broad area of your pursuit of true personal wealth. The other is the more specific area of your commitment to live out your life vision.

173

Your lifeWealth Team

True personal wealth results as we invest wisely in all five dimensions of lifeWealth capital. Therefore your support team will include the expertise of a number of individuals in each dimension. You have likely established a relationship with many of them already. But here are some suggestions:

Financial. Include on your team several key services to help you keep tabs on your financial affairs: financial planner, accountant, attorney, banker, and insurance agent. Interview candidates for these positions carefully. Understand how they are paid for their services. You don't necessarily want the least expensive service, but you can avoid paying unnecessary costs. I believe it is best to have one financial advisor who coordinates the efforts of the rest of your financial team.

Relational. A great many people define wealth in terms of having a great relationship with others, especially family members. I suggest that you get acquainted with a professional counselor even before you need any counseling. When relational conflicts arise, you will have someone on your team to help you work through them. If nothing else, identify someone who could serve as a trusted third party, such as a dear friend or your minister, to hear your conflicts and offer objective advice.

Physical. Your team starts with the medical doctor who quarterbacks your health team. Depending on your condition, you may need other specialists from time to time. You may also want to include a nutritionist and a physical trainer. At the very least, find someone who will walk, jog, or work out with you consistently. On the recreation side, consider taking a class just for fun.

Intellectual. Many individuals can help you develop new skills and polish the ones you already have. If you are a

EQUIP FOR SUCCESS

career person, consider adding a business coach or career counselor to your team. And you can find adult education classes on practically any subject.

Spiritual. Do you have someone on your team who is gifted and trained to assist you in your spiritual life? This could be a minister or a layperson who is mature in the faith. It is also important to settle into a place of worship where you are consistently taught how God relates to your life. And get involved with a small group of worshipers. Fellow believers will be an encouragement as you seek to know God.

Your Vision Team

Each of us also needs a team of people to help us stay on track and encouraged as we live out our vision. The more people you have around you to sharpen you, the more effective you will be. I'm not talking about merely an audience, people who watch and applaud your efforts from a distance; I'm talking about specific people you enlist to help you be the best you can be. And I'm not talking about people who simply rubber-stamp your efforts, but individuals you can count on for affirmation as well as direction and occasional correction. They are people you handpick and meet with periodically to help you stay sharp. Your support team may be enlisted from some or all of the following groups.

Close family members. Darrell's vision for influence is to utilize his gifts of leadership for helping his church remain healthy and grow. As such, he has volunteered for several committees and is annually reelected to the church board. Darrell is usually out two nights a week for committee or board meetings, and he spends one or two additional evenings discussing church business on the phone. And Darrell never misses a church service or Bible study meeting. All the church members appreciate Darrell's contribution of time and effort.

But Darrell's wife doesn't share their appreciation. Cindy doesn't like Darrell being away from home so many evenings. She has come to despise the church that has taken so much of her husband's time away from her and their children. But when she confronts Darrell about leaving for another meeting, he reminds her that he is merely using his abilities to serve the church. Cindy doesn't know how much longer she can endure playing second-string to Darrell's passion for church service.

If you are married, the first persons on your support team should be your spouse and children. Darrell is in danger of losing his wife and kids emotionally—and perhaps even physically—because he has not included them in his decisions about how much time he spends in church activities. No matter how clear your vision may be to you, your family should be on board and supportive of your direction. If they are not up to your speed, slow down and wait for them. It is better to move toward your vision at a slower speed than to leave those dearest to you in your wake.

As you are getting a clearer vision for your life, be sure you tell your spouse what you are learning about yourself. Your mate knows you better than anyone. He or she will be an excellent sounding board, and his or her vision may parallel yours. Share openly with each other and discover how you can journey together.

Accountability partners. I have been meeting for lunch nearly every week with Gary, Mike, and Tim for over twenty-three years. The purpose for our small group is simple: To care enough about each other to ask the tough questions. Author Tim Kimmel once asked his wife, Darcy, whom she would ask to be pallbearers at his funeral. When she couldn't answer him definitively, Tim determined that he needed to develop some deep, caring relationships with other men, or as he put it, he needed to begin grooming his pallbearers. My wife, Nancy, would put my three accountability buddies at the top of the list.

Next to Nancy and our children, these guys know more about me and my vision than anyone else on earth. They counsel me and hold me accountable for my actions—and I do the same for each of them. When I lose sight of my goal, when I get too full of myself, when I cop out of something I know I should do, my spiritual brothers lovingly hold my feet to the fire. And when I succeed, they are my biggest fans. They deserve at least part of the credit for anything of value I accomplish in the lives of those I desire to influence. I would not be living out my vision today if it were not for these guys on my team.

I suggest that you meet with this small core of people regularly, at least a couple times a month if not every week. Share your ongoing vision with each other, both the successes and failures. Affirm each other, encourage each other, and challenge each other to hang in there. One or two people in this category can make a huge difference in living out your vision.

Mentors and counselors. The original mentor was a friend of Odysseus entrusted with the education of Odysseus's son, Telemachus. The word *mentor* came to refer to a trusted counselor, guide, tutor, or coach. You are blessed if you can include a mentor on your support team, someone who has traveled the path you have chosen to travel and who is willing to share his or her knowledge and experience with you. Or a mentor may simply be someone who is more mature and wise about life in general. Whereas your friends are there to encourage you and hold you account-

177

able, a mentor is there to impart skills and coach you in developing them.

You may also want to seek out a professional counselor as an adjunct member of your support team. Counselors are trained to help you better see yourself and deal with any roadblocks keeping you from realizing your full potential. There are career counselors, spiritual counselors, and psychologists dealing with various elements of emotions and behavior. Consider scheduling periodic appointments with a professional who may be able to see your vision and yourself more clearly.

Balance Time and Priorities

When it comes to living out a life vision, we all have one major item in common. We all have twenty-four hours a day—no more, no less—to invest in fulfilling our purpose and passion. How we allocate the time determines our level of success. In order to equip yourself for success, you need to maintain a good balance between your available time and the priorities of your vision.

Let me illustrate from the financial world. As financial planners, my team and I must discover each client's investment priorities. Is the client looking for aggressive financial growth while maintaining a conservative base? Does he or she want to play it close to the vest with a minimum of risk? Is a middle-of-the-road strategy preferred? Every client has specific financial needs and goals. Each of them comes to us for a unique financial management strategy to meet those needs and achieve those goals.

Once we grasp the client's desires, we come up with what we call an "asset allocation model." In simplified terms, this strategy directs how much money goes into which investment instrument, based on the client's priorities.

After determining the proper allocation, we create a written "investment policy statement." The IPS becomes the framework for our strategies. It identifies the parameters for investing and the boundaries for decision making. Periodically we review the allocation model with the client and make any necessary adjustments in order to stay within the guidelines of the IPS.

However, seasons of the client's life and a variety of economic circumstances in the world sometimes prompt us to change the investment policy statement. We call such a change a "dynamic allocation," changing the IPS in order to adjust to external dynamics. Tracking with the IPS as a rule of thumb, and then altering it as necessary, is the way we maintain balance in the client's financial portfolio.

You can take a similar approach with respect to your life vision priorities and the time you have to invest. In this way you can compare and balance your priorities with your time commitments. Let's take a look at how this balance relates to a person we'll call Bill.

Bill would list the top priorities in his life in this order:

1. *Faith.* Bill has a strong faith and a desire to serve God.
2. *Family.* He has a wife, Deanna, two teenage daughters, and a preteen son. Next to God, they are Bill's highest priority.
3. *Vision.* The focus of Bill's life vision is the people of Haiti. He is committed to do what he can to bring hope to this island nation and help alleviate human suffering there.
4. *Work.* Bill is a masonry contractor with two full-time employees. Deanna is a part-time aide at a local

school, earning just a little above minimum wage. So Bill's income supports the family.

5. *Friends.* Bill and Deanna belong to a close-knit Bible study group at church, and they have a large group of friends and neighbors they socialize with.

6. *Health.* Having been in masonry for more than twenty years, Bill has back problems. He sees a specialist several times a year and must make sure he doesn't overdo it at work.

7. *Civic duties.* As a member of the elementary school board, Bill's pet project is better security in their community's three elementary schools.

8. *Recreation.* Left to himself, Bill would be a couch potato in his limited free time. His bad back rules out strenuous activities, so he watches sports on TV.

In an ideal world, Bill's time allocation would match his priority allocation in rank and proportions. In other words, his number one priority—his faith—would occupy more time than anything else, and so on down the list. But that rarely, if ever, happens in this world. Too much other stuff gets in the way. Circumstances arise beyond Bill's control. He must accommodate the needs of others. So in any given week—and on any given day in that week—his time allocation may look quite different from his priority allocation due to other influences in his life. Here's an example of what it could look like:

1. *Work.* Bill's job always occupies more of his time than anything else. He runs his crew during the day and bids jobs and does books in the evening. The only times this differs are when he takes a family vacation or flies to Haiti with a group of men from his church.

2. *Civic duties.* It doesn't happen very often, but this week Bill is logging several hours on school board responsibilities. The board is meeting two evenings and all day Saturday to hammer out a budget. Most weeks, civic duties are near the bottom of his time allocation.
3. *Family.* Despite his workload and the school board meetings, Bill is home for supper most evenings. And one night Bill was able to stay home and watch a movie with the family, one of their favorite activities together.
4. *Recreation.* Bill prefers to stay home and relax on Sundays after church. But this week his younger son's baseball team has a father-son picnic and softball game on Sunday afternoon. Bill even played an inning before his back started acting up. He had a good time, especially being with his son.
5. *Faith.* Because of school board meetings, Bill missed Bible study group, and the demanding schedule this week limited his time for Bible reading.
6. *Vision.* There hasn't been any time this week for Bill to work on his next trip to Haiti. He's thought about his work there several times and yearns for the day he can invest more of his time on a weekly basis.
7. *Health.* With life so busy, Bill has skipped his exercises and canceled a doctor's appointment.

Can you identify with Bill's experience? Of course you can! We live that way every week. Our priority allocation may remain basically the same from week to week. But our time allocation can change moment-to-moment and day-to-day as the circumstances of our lives change. Some weeks we must spend most of our time on things that are low priority. But that should not prevent us from working

181

toward the ideal of investing more of our time and energy in our higher priorities.

Time allocations sometimes change by the season of the year. Bill schedules at least one trip to Haiti every winter when construction work in his community has slowed down. The school board doesn't meet for two months during the summer, allowing Bill and his family to spend a week at church camp together. Time allocations can also change drastically over the seasons of life. The closer we get to the finish work phase, the more we should be able to control our time allocation, investing increasing amounts of time in our highest priorities, including vision.

It is also important to note that while Bill's faith is highest on his priority list, he doesn't always get to spend the amount of time directly involved in activities involving his faith. However, the way he cares for his family and how he conducts his business and relates to the community is directly impacted by how he lives out his faith. Sometimes we compartmentalize so much that we miss those connections.

The key to success in this ongoing reshuffling between time and priorities is balance. Remember the tips for life juggling we discussed earlier in the book? They apply well to the seeming incompatibility between our priorities and available time. Just because you can't invest time in your priorities this week—or month or year or decade—as you would like, continue to keep things in balance. Invest what you must in lower-priority activities. Invest what you can in higher-priority activities. The seasons will change and you will find yourself moving toward greater fulfillment in your vision.

Whether you are investing yourself and your time in high- or low-priority activities, one strategy will greatly determine the kind of return you receive on that investment. In the next chapter we will explore the importance of generosity as you live out your vision.

Small Change *Challenges*

- "To be the best you can be as you journey the path of influence, you must equip yourself continually for success." Make a list of some specific vector changes that you should consider to become more prepared for opportunities that come your way.
- What action can you take immediately that will initiate proactive living?

12

Give from the Heart

———————•———————

In their book *The Generosity Factor,* Ken Blanchard and C. Truett Cathy use fiction to present a foundational principle for business and all of life. In the story, a very successful executive shares the secret of his success with a power-hungry, money-driven broker.

"Here they are," the Executive finally continued slowly and deliberately, as if he were expecting the Broker to take notes on his little electronic device. "Time. Talent. Treasure. Touch. Nothing more than these four. The beauty of it is, there are so many ways to give them. The tragedy is that so few people discover ways to give one—let alone four."

The Broker thought about this for a moment. "I can understand how someone in your position could give treasure, but I can't understand giving anything beyond that. You and I are over-extended business people with responsibilities to our employees and customers. I know that in my position, I could never give time or talent. How is it that you can?"

It seemed as though the Executive had somehow anticipated the question and was ready with his answer. "I've lived many years and enjoyed so many blessings. And I believe that because much has been given to me, I owe much in return. I also believe that we can all find time to do the things we enjoy. I enjoy discovering ways to meet the needs of others, so I make time for that."

Is this all talk, or does he actually invest his time? the broker wondered.

The Executive interrupted his thoughts. "You're wondering if I actually do that."

"Well, yes. How did you know?"

"A lot of folks say they care about people, but they don't actually do anything about it. Generosity is all about caring about the needs of others, then acting to meet those needs. Time meets a certain kind of need. Talent meets another. Treasure still another, and touch meets its own set of needs. Generosity is about balance—about making all of one's resources available."[1]

A key strategy for acquiring true personal wealth is to give generously to others from what you have. Sounds like a contradiction, doesn't it? How can you *acquire* anything by *giving*? You must remember that true personal wealth is more about realizing deep fulfillment and satisfaction than about accumulating things. The more generous you are with what you have, the richer you will become in possessions no one can ever take from you.

Jesus uttered the familiar words, "It is more blessed to give than to receive."[2] In another discussion about giving and abundance, he clarified that statement: "If you give, you will receive. Your gift will return to you in full measure, pressed down, shaken together to make room for more, and running over. Whatever measure you use in giving—large or small—it will be used to measure what is given back to you."[3]

186

What can we give? I think Blanchard and Cathy have captured it well in their story with the four key elements listed by the Executive. Generosity begins with an attitude of willingness to invest yourself in others in these four general areas.

Time. As we discussed in the last chapter, everyone has twenty-four hours a day, seven days a week, fifty-two weeks a year. For most of us, significant chunks of our time are already committed. It's our discretionary time—that final eight hours, so to speak—that we're talking about. How much of my free time will I invest in others? And how much of my committed time can be converted to discretionary time through wise planning and careful use?

Talent. We all have an abundant supply of this, too, though it differs greatly from person to person. You have natural God-given abilities, a unique personality, your IQ, spiritual gifts, and the skills you have acquired through education and job training. Your various talents may bring you a level of satisfaction and even profit. But I believe our talents pay the greatest personal dividends when we invest them in others.

Treasure. We are probably more different in this category than any other. Depending on a number of factors, you are somewhere on the scale between very wealthy and poverty-stricken. But generosity is not related to how much or how little you have; it's about your attitude toward what you *do* have. Visiting the temple one day, Jesus called his disciples' attention to those who brought offerings. The account reads, "Many rich people put in large amounts. Then a poor widow came and dropped in two pennies. He called his disciples to him and said, 'I assure you, this poor widow has given more than all the others have given. For they gave a tiny part of their surplus, but she, poor as she is, has given everything she has.'"[4]

We all came into the world with a zero balance financially and materially—and we leave the same way. Everything we possess we have received from others, most notably from God, who gave us the smarts and strength to acquire what we have. Since nothing really belongs to us, the attitude and actions of generosity, as exemplified by the poor widow, are the only reasonable response to our treasure.

Touch. I believe we are all endowed with an unlimited supply of human compassion. We have great capacity to be generous with our love, kindness, and caring for others. And it's a good thing, too, because the people around us need warm, welcoming handshakes, affirming words, friendly pats on the back, and comforting embraces. Sadly, human compassion often gets buried under self-centeredness. We are stingy instead of lavishing on others our helping, healing touch.

Generosity is a grace that supercedes our unique abilities and life vision. In other words, it's right to be generous to others whether or not we feel particularly gifted or called to do so. We need to strive for excellence in our act of giving as if it were a competition that requires our best efforts and preparation.

In this chapter I want to talk about two applications of generosity on the path of influence. The first is quite broad, exploring our investment of financial, relational, physical, intellectual, and spiritual capital in general. The second is rather specific, zeroing in on giving ourselves to others in mentoring relationships. In both cases, generosity is an expression of the heart through which we invest deeply in others.

Investing All Dimensions of lifeWealth Capital

A giving heart is ready to expend time, talent, treasure, and touch in order to effect positive influence on other people. What might these expenditures look like across the five dimensions of lifeWealth capital?

Financial Capital

The way we spend our money reveals what is important to us. In response to a poor widow's small but selfless contribution, Jesus said, "Where your treasure is, there your heart will be also."[5] Generosity in the area of financial capital is pretty obvious—investing our material treasure in other people, not to reap a financial return but to contribute, as much as we are able, something positive and helpful to someone else. As Jesus' comment indicates, the amount is not as important as the attitude.

Here's a simple example of how someone's generosity can make a little money go a long way. Cheryl and Ted love shopping at garage sales. Most Saturday mornings during the spring and summer months you can find this retired couple crisscrossing their community in search of cast-off treasures for sale. Cheryl looks for collectibles: glass, lace doilies and tablecloths, knickknacks. But Ted looks for kids who are selling cookies or donuts or lemonade at their parents' garage sales. When he finds enterprising young vendors, Ted asks them how sales are going, buys whatever they are selling, and compliments them on how well they're doing. You can see the positive impact as their eyes light up. Ted isn't there to buy snacks; he's there to encourage the kids in their financial ventures. And it only costs him a few quarters a week.

Here are several more ideas for expressing generosity through your financial capital:

• Contribute regularly to your house of worship.

189

- Put your change in those checkout stand receptacles for disease research.
- Support fund-raisers for worthy causes.
- Donate unused clothing to shelters for the homeless.
- Sponsor kids for church camp.
- Buy gifts of appreciation for people who serve you: mail carrier, newspaper delivery person, baby-sitter, and others.
- Tip generously.
- Contribute to the scholarship fund of your alma mater.

Relational Capital

Investing yourself relationally encompasses everything you have: time, talent, treasure, and touch. Since we have already talked about treasure and will talk about talent under intellectual capital, I would like to focus on the other two: time and touch.

Time. A lot has been said about the importance of investing "quality time" in people over "quantity time." I might buy that argument if I was convinced we could control what happens during quality time. But we can't. For example, you sit down with your teenage daughter for twenty minutes of conversation. You have designated it quality time because you plan to ask how it's going at school and with her friends. But if you get twenty minutes of "It's OK," "Yeah, I guess," "I don't know," "I don't know," and "I don't know," where's the quality?

Don't let anybody mislead you with the lie that quality time with people is better than quantity time. In reality, quality comes out of quantity. When we invest time generously in our family members, friends, coworkers, and neighbors, we come across gold nuggets of close connection and deep interaction. I saw this played out so many times with my children. When I sat them down intending to "make quality happen," it usually didn't. But when one of the kids and I were out running errands or attending a ball game or working on their homework, we often ended up enjoying some quality moments together.

My good friend Bill Mutz owns a car dealership in Florida. He and his wife, Pam, are on the FamilyLife speaking team with Nancy and me. This couple is active in their church and in several civic groups. They invest their time in quality endeavors, impacting many people in their community and across the nation. But here's the amazing thing: Bill and Pam have twelve children!

Nancy and I were recently in their home for an evening. We watched with amazement as these parents gave each child focused attention. None of them seemed to lack parental love and affection. I overheard a conversation between Bill and one of his sons about rescheduling a breakfast date that had been missed because Bill and Pam had been at a conference. The calendar came out and breakfast was rescheduled, to the boy's delight.

Bill told me that each child gets a one-on-one breakfast date with Dad each month. It's a special time for each child and for Bill. Some breakfast dates are spent in casual conversation, while other chats get deep into the heart of issues a child is facing. Bill doesn't often determine what will happen. He is simply committed to spending time with his kids, allowing memorable, lasting conversations to unfold naturally.

Most of us are very busy, and our time is at a premium. It's a daily challenge to allot our time to those who need it. I encourage you to keep working for balance between your time and priority allocations, as discussed in the last chapter. When you must choose between priorities, be sure your prime targets for influence—especially family members—are not ignored.

Touch. Let's talk about investing in others by connecting through conversation. I've noticed two kinds of people when it comes to making conversation: tellers and askers. Tellers use the conversation as an opportunity to tell what they know, share their stories, and state their opinions. When the other person is talking, tellers are quietly planning what they're going to say next instead of listening with interest. They are just waiting for the other person to take a breath so they can jump in. When two tellers get together, it may seem more like dueling monologues than a give-and-take conversation.

Askers ask at least as much as they tell. They are in the conversation to demonstrate genuine interest in the other person and draw him or her out. You'll hear them say such things as: "What's the latest on your job search?" "Tell me about your trip to Mexico." "How did you meet your spouse?" "When did your faith really come alive?" "What do you think about what's happening in the stock market?" "Tell me about your kids." "How did you decide to decorate your house?" When you get two askers together, you usually get a meaningful, connecting conversation. Each touches the other with caring interest.

Becoming an asker is a prime way to invest yourself in others. People are encouraged when someone draws them out, listens to what they say, and demonstrates genuine interest. And you have many opportunities each day to extend this kind of generosity in all your relationships. This is a skill that can be learned. Nancy and I have seen the value of this in so many relationships, which is why we taught the skill to our children with the "five question rule."

Physical Capital

Jack was a star basketball player in high school, a prime candidate for a college scholarship. But being the eldest of nine children in a working-class home, Jack had to go to work to help his dad support the family. He still hoped he could play college ball someday. But within a couple of years, Jack joined the army, got married, and started a family of his own. He never made it to college.

Even though his dream of college ball was never realized, Jack learned to share his love and skill for basketball with others. As his two sons grew up, he coached their youth basketball teams. Jack also organized and participated in church basketball teams. Recently Jack bought season tickets for the college team in town, and he enjoys taking other guys with him. And he still loves a pick-up game once in a while. Jack has experienced the satisfaction and fulfillment of investing physical capital—in his case, his love of basketball—in others.

What are your prime strengths in the areas of health, wellness, and recreation? How could you generously share those attributes for others' benefit? Your investment of physical capital may look something like one of these suggestions:

- Make yourself available to help move furniture for elderly neighbors in need of a strong back.
- Take somebody to the gym with you and teach him or her how to use the equipment.
- Share your healthiest recipes with family members and friends.
- Coach a sports team for your kids and their friends.

Intellectual Capital

Della is a craftsperson. She is especially skilled at creating elegant handmade greeting cards, gift boxes and bags, holiday wreaths, and many other crafts. But her greatest joy is teaching crafts classes to small groups of women in her church and community and seeing others awaken their artistic skills. Della also enjoys the camaraderie that develops when a group of women work and play together for two hours.

Burt teaches fifth grade, but he is also a gifted Mr. Fix-it, skilled in plumbing, electrical, carpentry, and painting. His best buddy, Don, is a journalist and all-thumbs when it comes to household repairs. Whenever Don has a project, such as installing a light fixture or repairing a leaky faucet, Burt always comes over to help—which usually means he does the job while Don hands him tools.

Kevin is an outdoorsman. Every summer he spends a week of his vacation leading a backpacking trip for members of the church youth group, for which he and his wife serve as volunteer sponsors. On each trip, Kevin, Janna, and the adult leaders they recruit teach the kids about plants and animals in the region and show them how to cook over a campfire. Kevin loves to hike and backpack with Janna, but he gladly shares his experience and vacation time to introduce youth to the great outdoors.

Regina is a successful tax accountant with a waiting list of clients. Yet every Friday afternoon during tax season you will find her at the community center helping migrant workers fill out their tax forms—pro bono. Regina knows these people will never be paying customers, but it is important to her to use her skills to help the less fortunate.

Generosity with intellectual capital means sharing your talents with others. What are your unique abilities? What specific skills have you acquired and honed over the years?

True, your gifts, skills, and abilities may be the way you make your living. But how can you use those special talents to bless others without charge? You will likely find that the abilities you share with others from the heart will bring you more personal satisfaction than the paycheck and prestige they earn you.

My friend Mike Colby is one of my accountability partners. We have known each other since seventh grade. Mike is very proficient as a fix-it guy. He enjoys the challenge of a project. I, on the other hand, am "fix-it challenged." I own several tools, mainly because they look good in my garage! I don't even know what half of them are for.

One January several years ago, Mike and his wife, Linda, came over to watch the Super Bowl with us. Mike doesn't appreciate sports like I do, so after a short time, he disappeared. After a while, I went looking for him and found him in our basement. In his hand was the "honey do" list that Nancy puts on our refrigerator door. (I'm still not sure why she puts it there; she knows how inept I am at household repairs.) Mike had decided to dive into my list and complete some of the projects. That's a true friend! Since then, when I know Mike and Linda are coming over, I quickly get my list in order in hopes that he will feel motivated again to be Mr. Fix-it. Mike is an excellent example of someone being generous with his intellectual capital.

Spiritual Capital

There is an interesting twist to extending generosity from the spiritual dimension of our lives. God doesn't need our treasure or our talents, even though we can share these elements with others in his name. What he wants is us—the whole package of who we are, no strings attached. God invites us to surrender our lives to him completely in order to experience the ultimate in satisfaction and fulfillment through an intimate relationship with the God who made us, loves us unconditionally, and longs to fill our lives with himself.

Spiritual intimacy doesn't go very deep if we are stingy with God. One way to demonstrate our generosity to him is with our time, perhaps our most precious commodity. Give him time at the beginning of each day through prayer and Bible reading. Be sure to set aside one day a week—Sunday is perhaps the best day—to rest from work and charge your spiritual batteries in fellowship with others. It's difficult to connect with God unless we slow down, quiet down, and listen to him. Our Creator invites us to "be still, and know that I am God."[6]

Generosity across the lifeWealth dimensions must move beyond the "good idea" stage to do any good. Simply agreeing that generosity is a noble virtue and thinking about ways you can be a generous person isn't enough. Generosity requires action. It's something you can do every day, something you can even schedule on your daily planner. Don't wait until you have more time, talent, or treasure to share with others. Learn to be generous with what you have now, little though it may be, and you are well on your way to being generous with much, if and when you have it.

Focusing Your Generosity through Mentoring

Mentoring is the generous, concentrated investment of your capital in the lives of specific people. Mentoring is a personalized strategy for teaching, coaching, and encouraging others in certain skills or disciplines. Remember Andrea from chapter 9, the career woman with a heart for helping other women deal with the challenges of family and career? Those six-month sessions were a concentrated, individualized dose of her generosity.

While we experience great fulfillment in expressing generosity toward God and others in all areas of daily life, mentoring zooms in on specific opportunities for sustained generosity with certain individuals. Mentoring is a focus of time and priority. Those you mentor will likely rank fairly high in your time/priority allocations for a certain period. Mentoring is a focus of talents. You are not trying to impart everything to those you mentor but zeroing in on your greatest strengths and unique abilities.

Here are a few more examples of mentoring relationships:

- Carlos meets for breakfast weekly with three men from church who want to learn more about God. In between meetings, each participant completes a worksheet on the topic of the week. Carlos leads the discussion and answers questions.
- Several employees in Frieda's office struggle with the software program they all use. Frieda offers to coach any who desire personalized help with the software. She usually meets with a coworker for two or three lunch hours before that person feels confident. Frieda remains available to those she coaches after the personalized sessions.
- Buck played a couple years of minor league baseball before blowing out his knee and ending his career. Every spring he offers a fielding clinic for eight-year-olds through his community's Little League. He teaches the fundamentals of throwing, catching, and handling ground balls. During the season he hangs around the park to work individually with players who ask for help.

- Ellie volunteers at her son's school three days each week. She especially enjoys tutoring struggling readers. She takes on two students, usually from different classes, and reads with each of them for an hour.

Your possibilities for mentoring are only limited by your abilities and your willingness to give of yourself and your time. The following steps may help you decide where and how you can become a mentor.

Identify your mentoring strengths. Obviously you will experience greater success and fulfillment if you coach, teach, or tutor others out of your strengths. This should bring you right back to your unique abilities and your passions. What are your best transferable skills? In other words, what are you particularly good at that others can learn and profit from? What knowledge have you acquired with time and experience that might help you shorten the learning curve for others? What do you get excited to see others learn and apply to their lives? These questions should lead you to one or two areas of personal strength from which you can mentor others.

Offer your strengths to others. You cannot force your coaching on others. Somehow you need to communicate to those in need of your strengths that you are available and willing to share your knowledge and experience with them. Do you know people who struggle in areas in which you are strong? Have others come to you asking for your advice, insight, or instruction in some area? Have you noticed an unmet need in your workplace, church, or community that seems to be crying out for your expertise? With just a little thought, you can probably come up with a list of possible candidates for your mentoring.

Decide how much you can provide. Since you have other time and priority allocations in your life, you must decide how much you can do and how many people you can mentor at any one time. It is important to filter your mentoring options through your top priorities. Talk to your spouse and children about what you hope to do and make sure they are comfortable with the time you will direct toward mentoring. Ask God to give you wisdom for making the tough calls about how much time and talent you can devote to this rewarding experience.

Enlist your first participants. Keep talking with the candidates you have identified until a sufficient number have responded. Decide how many you can mentor at one time and under what circumstances. Keep in contact with those who may be interested but cannot be included at first.

Establish limits. Don't jeopardize other life priorities by taking on more mentoring than you can effectively do. This applies to the number of people you can help and the amount of time you will invest in each one. Establish a time frame—six months, five meetings, a year of meeting monthly. At the end of that period, evaluate the situation and either continue or conclude as you see fit. Setting limits at the outset helps others realize that you aren't signing on to mentor them for life.

If you resist the idea of being generous with your time, talent, treasures, and touch, it's probably because you don't fully appreciate how others have helped and encouraged you. An attitude of generosity springs from a thankful heart. And we can only be thankful when we step back and count our blessings. Take inventory of your life and notice what you have. Then realize how little it would be without the help of God and many others who generously helped you get where you are.

If you cling tightly to what you have instead of opening up to share with others, your heart is like a clenched fist, holding everything for yourself. But with a clenched fist, you can't receive anything else. You are closed to other good things that may come your way. But if you walk through life with an open-handed attitude, ready to share generously who you are and what you have, you're in a great position to receive and enjoy even more. Don't let a miserly heart rob you of all that life has to offer. Open up, share generously, and enjoy life.

Small Change *Challenges*

- "A key strategy for acquiring true personal wealth is to give generously to others from what you have." List some specific ways you could give some of your time, talent, treasure, and touch to others.
- Think of someone who needs you to give generously. What does he or she need from you and what can you do *now* to meet that need?

13

Enjoy the Journey

—— ———— • ————

The journey to influence and true personal wealth is not an uninterrupted magic carpet ride to ultimate success and fulfillment. As an imperfect person dwelling in an imperfect world, even your best attempts at living out your vision will fall short of perfection. Your purpose may be clear and your passions pure, but the road between where you are now and journey's end has some jarring potholes, dangerous curves, black ice, and surprise dead ends.

For one thing, you will mess up along the way because everybody messes up. We are all subject to mistakes, self-ishness, impatience, intolerance, greed, hatred, jealousy, laziness, envy—you know what I'm talking about, don't you? And our imperfections and shortcomings sometimes temporarily distract us, divert us, detour us, or derail us on the journey.

For another thing, life around us doesn't always play out the way we expect, let alone the way we plan. Circumstances slip beyond our control. People as imperfect as we are let us down, tear us down, refuse to cooperate, and block our progress in some way—whether intentionally or unintentionally. Let's face it: Life is tough. The path to true personal wealth is an uphill climb most of the way.

But don't get me wrong. The satisfaction of seeing people enriched and transformed through your efforts is well worth the difficulties of the journey. The joy of exercising your unique abilities and seeing others grow as a result certainly overshadows the pain you may experience in the process. You need a standard other than perfection, stunning achievement, or unbridled success by which to evaluate your journey. Such qualities are good *desires,* but they are feeble *standards of measurement,* because people and circumstances can block you from achieving them.

You need a standard that cannot be blocked from the outside, something you can achieve by yourself. I suggest that your daily standard be to enjoy the journey and find contentment where you are at the moment.

Before we discuss what contentment *is,* let's understand what it is *not.*

First, contentment is not *resignation.* When the going gets tough on the road to true personal wealth, the paths of indulgence or indifference suddenly look easy and fun. At times you will be tempted to give up. And if you do give up, you may indeed experience a measure of relief. Having taken yourself out of the battle, you may feel content because no one is knocking you around anymore.

But if you bail out of your circumstances to find contentment, what happens to your vision? It goes to the sidelines with you. You're no longer in pursuit of true personal wealth; you're just sitting on the bench trying to avoid pain. You don't have to resign from the journey to find contentment. True contentment is available in the midst of the journey, even when it's difficult.

202

Second, contentment is not *complacency*. Complacency is self-satisfaction, the attitude that whatever you did or whatever resulted may be subpar but it's good enough for you. That's a compromise of vision, giving up on yourself or settling for less than your best effort. Contentment doesn't mean selling out to mediocrity. Rather, it's a peaceful posture in the midst of a strong effort, even if the results are less than what you hoped for.

Third, contentment is not *indifference*, the absence of emotion, concern, ambition, and drive. Contentment doesn't shrug and say, "I don't care." To the contrary, contentment is full of heart and caring, even in the heat of the battle, in the face of defeat, or on the brink of despair. And there is plenty of room for ambition, drive, determination, and hard work as you experience contentment. You do not have to slip into emotional neutral to be content.

There is a lot written about contentment, but it is best understood and learned when we see it modeled. Nobody I know of has modeled contentment more effectively than the person I'd like to introduce you to.

A Case Study in Contentment

Saul was known for his laser-focused vision, heartfelt passion, life-changing influence, crushing setbacks, and unparalleled contentment. He was the consummate type A, driven and goal oriented even before he set foot on the path of influence. Charging down the path of indulgence at top speed, he didn't care who got in his way. Anyone between him and his goal was bowled over. He single-handedly rocked the world around him.

Then in one blinding flash, he hit bottom. Suddenly aware of the error of his ways, he was man enough to change. The same passion and drive that had fueled his misguided quest now helped launch him in a positive new direction. However, Saul had made a lot of enemies in the past, and his midlife course change to a path of influence garnered a lot of opposition. But he wasn't about to back down. If anything, he was even more passionate about being on the right road, despite those who wanted to take him out.

The abuse he suffered was horrendous. It was physical and brutal. His enemies nearly killed him more than once. But every time he got knocked down, he found a way to get up and keep going. And here's the most amazing thing: He was totally content with his lot. Despite painful, life-threatening opposition, he never wavered, never gave up. No bellyaching, no whining, no wishing for the old days. He had found a secret inner strength, and that was all the contentment he needed.

Saul is also known as the apostle Paul, to whom I have referred a number of times in this book. You can read about his dramatic turnaround, when his name changed from Saul to Paul, in Acts 9 of the New Testament.

After a life-changing experience,[1] Paul set his course for a life of influencing others and never looked back. His purpose and passion merged into a compelling vision.

Paul possessed a rock-solid inner strength completely independent of his circumstances—contentment. This core element allowed him to view both triumphant victories and crushing defeats with a level head and a peaceful heart. And he was happy to share his secret with others. During his last imprisonment before being executed for his faith, he wrote:

> I have learned to be content whatever the circumstances. I know what it is to be in need, and I know what it is to have plenty. I have learned the secret of being content in any and every situation, whether well fed or hungry, whether living

204

in plenty or in want. I can do everything through him who gives me strength.[2]

In another of his letters, Paul lets us know that contentment is available to everyone: "God is able to make all grace abound to you, so that in all things at all times, having all that you need, you will abound in every good work."[3] Interestingly, the phrase "having all that you need" comes from a form of the Greek word Paul uses in the Philippians passage and elsewhere for "contentment." We could paraphrase the verse, "God is able to make all grace abound to you, so that in all things at all times, *being content,* you will abound in every good work." Contentment allows you to keep moving forward no matter what life may throw at you. Contentment helps you enjoy the journey even when some of your experiences are less than enjoyable.

Guidelines for Growing in Contentment

It is difficult to achieve contentment in a culture in which enough is never enough and more is always better. The blaring campaign to spend, accumulate, and consume dominates our economy and fuels the advertising media. The credo of business is to climb the corporate ladder, trounce the competition, and be the best you can be at any cost. Status quo has become a four-letter word. Why settle for where you are if you can go higher or further—and do it faster than anyone else? Why be content with what you have when you can upgrade to something newer, fancier, more prestigious, or state-of-the-art? After all, look at the generous limit on our credit cards!

How do you incorporate Paul's brand of contentment in such a world as ours? Let me provide a few ideas by considering once again the five dimensions of lifeWealth.

Financial Contentment

When you read Paul's comments about contentment in the area of money and possessions, you might wonder if he had special insight into twenty-first-century culture. In reality, he had insight into the universal desire for more. He wrote to his protégé Timothy:

> For we brought nothing into the world, and we can take nothing out of it. But if we have food and clothing, we will be content with that. People who want to get rich fall into temptation and a trap and into many foolish and harmful desires that plunge men into ruin and destruction. For the love of money is a root of all kinds of evil. Some people, eager for money, have wandered from the faith and pierced themselves with many griefs.[4]

Notice that Paul isn't against having money. He doesn't even condemn being rich. His words are often misquoted as "Money is the root of all kinds of evil." No, money isn't the problem; it's the *love* of money and stuff—the seemingly insatiable craving for more—that can get us into trouble. And being rich isn't the problem; it's the consuming drive for riches that puts us on a slippery slope. I believe Paul's formula for success in the material world is to put God first and be content with what you have—be it little or much.

What are your top financial and material desires? A dream house with every feature you have always wanted? Your own successful business? An early retirement to travel and play golf? A college education for your kids? A new SUV every two years? How content would you feel if your dreams came true?

Now, there is nothing wrong with these kinds of desires, nor is it wrong to work hard to achieve them. But you have no guarantees that your efforts will reap the rewards you desire. Too many things can go wrong, things you can't control, such as the economy and your health. Can you be content on each step of your financial journey, even if your dreams are never realized?

When you can experience the same contentment with little or much, you are in a great position to funnel more of your material resources to meet the needs of others. Nothing is wrong with a new SUV every two years, but if you kept your car for six years, how much good could you do with the money you save? And perhaps your dream home can still be dreamy if you compromise on some features in order to help meet someone else's material dreams. Financial contentment at all stages opens up many opportunities for investing your resources in the lives of others.

Relational Contentment

When Barry was transferred across country, his life didn't change much. He still logged forty to fifty hours each week at the new plant and spent part of each weekend in the study at home on paperwork. But the move was a major adjustment for his wife, Debi. Back home she had thrived in several active social circles: a neighborhood coffee group, her coworkers at the office, her pinochle group, and a few close friends who were like sisters. But all of these relationships were now twenty-eight hundred miles away. For Debi, no amount of e-mails, phone calls, and letters could fill the void of missing the people she used to see on a daily or weekly basis. And soon even the correspondence from home began to diminish.

Debi and Barry didn't realize how difficult it would be to establish social connections in a place where they knew virtually no one. A few neighbors waved hello but never came over to meet them. The couple began attending a large, friendly church, but the members were so busy being friendly to each other that newcomers like Debi and Barry were overlooked. Debi found a part-time job doing what she did back home, but it was tough breaking into the office clique. Evenings at home were the hardest. Debi's former swirling social life had calmed to few phone calls, fewer evenings out with people, and a constant cloud of loneliness.

As Debi discovered, our relational capital can sometimes be as difficult to control as our financial capital. As much as we may wish it didn't happen, family members die; friends move away; coworkers quit, get transferred, or retire; and relationships of all kinds dissolve due to conflict or misunderstanding. Those who enjoy a few lifetime friendships and positive long-term relationships are truly blessed.

How does someone in Debi's situation find relational contentment? I think it starts with the bare necessities, just as learning to be content with food and clothing is the foundation for financial contentment. Relational contentment begins with three basic elements.

1. You need a mentor. You need a mentor in your life, at least one trusted, mature individual who is willing to share his or her guidance, wisdom, advice, and instruction with you. I would counsel Debi to develop a relationship with a wise woman, someone with a healthy marriage, a strong faith, and a willingness to serve others. If you are not in relationship with a "life coach," I think you are missing one of the bare necessities for relational contentment.

2. You need a friend. Along with a wise mentor, you need a committed friend among your relationships, a Mr. or Ms. Encouragement in your life. A friend is someone with whom you can be yourself. When you're up, your friend celebrates with you. When you're down, your friend toughs it out with you. It may take Debi a while in her new locale to cultivate the kind of close friendships she left behind, but as they say, to have a friend you must be a friend. She will have to make an effort to meet some women and get acquainted.

In the meantime, Debi has Barry. If you're married, your spouse should fill the role of your closest soul mate, as Nancy and I do for each other. Beyond that I suggest that you develop at least one deep, encouraging friendship with someone of your sex. I have found this strong bond in the three friends I have met with for lunch for more than twenty years.

3. *You need a protégé.* Another bare essential for contentment in a life of influence is at least one relationship in which you are a source of influence to someone into whom you can pour your life. Debi should have no trouble finding someone to teach or coach in her new church. If nothing else, there is likely a Sunday school class in which Debi can help guide girls or young women. Do you have a protégé in your life, someone you are mentoring or coaching in some area?

Three vital relationships that will help you enjoy the journey: a mentor to input to your life, a friend for mutual encouragement, and a disciple to coach. Of course, these are just the bare essentials. I trust that wherever you go, you will link up with a number of people in each category.

Physical Contentment

It is reasonable to hope and expect that our financial and relational capital will continue to grow throughout our lifetime. We all dream of finishing life with a bulging financial portfolio to pass on to others and a wealth of wonderful relationships. However, it is unreasonable to hope and expect for unending improvement in the area of physical capital. At some point during the framework phase of our lives, we reach a point of diminishing returns. As the body ages, it just can't perform as well in some areas as it used to. Consider, for example, that the majority of world-class athletes are in their teens and twenties. Age thirty-five is considered over-the-hill in many sports. Even a fortysomething runner in excellent physical condition would be outclassed by a twenty-five-year-old in similar condition.

The aging process catches up with all of us. When I was younger, if I made up my mind to get into shape, a few days at the gym and watching what I ate would make a noticeable difference in my physique. These days, weeks of intensive workouts and strict dieting make little difference in how I look. My strategy is more about maintaining what I have than getting back to where I was twenty years ago.

If you are in your thirties or older, what do you think as you see yourself slowly turn wrinkled and gray—whether you are successful at hiding it or not? If you are in your forties or fifties, how does it feel to be passed up for a promotion by a younger, stronger, better-educated employee? How do you handle it when your kids or grandkids can beat you in a footrace, pin you to the floor during a friendly wrestling match, or even outjump you in a game of checkers? Unless you come to terms with the aging process, you will find it increasingly difficult to be content about your physical condition as the years roll by.

Contentment in any area of lifeWealth capital is never a product of comparison to others. You will always find someone who is wealthier than you are, has more friends than you do, or can pump more iron than you can. Even worse is to compare yourself with what you could do five or ten years ago.

Physical contentment comes from knowing what you can do now and operating comfortably within that zone. I know about an eighty-two-year-old woman who is facing both hip and knee replacement surgery due to severe arthritis. Annie can no longer bowl or square-dance as she did in her younger years. But she is content to stay as physically fit as she is able. She watches what she eats, and three or four mornings a week she drives to the gym for a water aerobics class. She doesn't like being hindered by arthritis, but she doesn't let that stop her from being content.

Since we are talking about a *life* of influence, I believe it is important to do whatever we can to sustain a long, healthy life. The longer you live and the healthier you remain, the more people you will be able to benefit through your unique abilities and vision for influence. So enjoy the journey by eating right, exercising regularly, and resting well. And continue to invest your life in others as your physical strength and ability allow.

Intellectual Contentment

Many things can rob you of contentment in the area of your intellectual capital. It is vital that you identify these thieves and neutralize them, because your talents and gifts are primary for investing in and positively influencing others. Here are three things that disrupt the joy of the journey for many people.

Diminished abilities. As with physical capital, time, progress, and the aging process have a way of eroding some of our intellectual abilities. The person who came into the company with the best skills and education available at the time is now passed up by employees with advanced training and degrees. The youth club volunteer who relates well to kids in her twenties and thirties may lose touch with them in her forties. The line worker who can assemble twenty widgets an hour may see that number dwindle with time. Some of our abilities may continue to improve with time, but others may diminish, causing us to wonder if we are losing our usefulness.

Focus your energy and attention on using those abilities that improve with age instead of worrying that you are not as skilled or successful as you used to be in other areas.

A deflated view of your abilities. Penny, a widow in her late fifties, has a heart for young women who are pregnant and considering abortion. She volunteers at the pregnancy counseling center in her community, doing data entry. Penny sees many girls come in for pregnancy testing and counseling. She would enjoy one-on-one contact with some of these girls, but social skills are not Penny's strength. So she stays at the computer and often views her role as menial compared to what the counselors get to do.

Like Penny, a lot of people view their abilities as second-class. They see people in high-profile positions with great responsibility and think their own contributions are unimportant. Paul has a problem with that line of thinking. In one of his letters, the apostle compares the various roles in the church to the parts of a human body. Notice what he says to those who think their smaller, less glamorous role is less important:

> If the foot should say, "Because I am not a hand, I do not belong to the body," it would not for that reason cease to be part of the body. And if the ear should say, "Because I am not an eye, I do not belong to the body," it would not for that reason cease to be part of the body. If the whole body were an eye, where would the sense of hearing be? If the whole body were an ear, where would the sense of smell be?

212

But in fact God has arranged the parts in the body, every one of them, just as he wanted them to be. If they were all one part, where would the body be?[5]

The point is clear. No matter how small or insignificant your gifts and abilities seem to you, they are just as important as anyone else's. Penny's skill at data entry is vital to the ongoing success of the pregnancy counseling center. Without her constantly updated files, some of the young women Penny desperately wants to help may slip through the cracks. Similarly, your small, gifted part is vital to the whole. Don't underestimate or devalue what God has wired you to do.

An inflated view of your abilities. On the other side of the scale from people like Penny are those who see their special abilities as more important than those of others. This often happens to people with "high visibility" gifts: leaders, public speakers, others who work in the spotlight instead of behind the scenes. Sometimes these individuals are so impressed with their own abilities that they cause others to feel unneeded.

Continuing with the illustration of the human body, Paul speaks pointedly to this wrong view.

As it is, there are many parts, but one body.

The eye cannot say to the hand, "I don't need you!" And the head cannot say to the feet, "I don't need you!" On the contrary, those parts of the body that seem to be weaker are indispensable, and the parts that we think are less honorable we treat with special honor. . . . But God has combined the members of the body and has given greater honor to the parts that lacked it, so that there should be no division in the body, but that its parts should have equal concern for each other.[6]

Intellectual contentment results as you accept your God-given abilities and carry out your role wholeheartedly as if doing it for God.

Spiritual Contentment

I believe spiritual contentment comes from acknowledging that we are in a growth process.

We should always be growing and maturing in our relationship with God. You may not know as much about God today as you would like. You may feel inadequate when it comes to prayer and understanding the Bible. But these things will come in time as long as you keep "eating"—learning more about God and practicing what you learn—and growing. Instead of lamenting that you have so far yet to go, glance back and see how far you have come already. Be content with the progress you are making instead of moping about your imperfections.

Your journey along the path of influence may be difficult and challenging at times, but it shouldn't be dismal and depressing. It can and should be a journey of contentment and even joy. Yet contentment and joy on the journey is a choice, one we can make daily and so enjoy the journey.

Small Change *Challenges*

- Describe your greatest disappointment in life.
- Think about that disappointment and what part of it you can change. Make a plan for the necessary vector changes to correct the situation. If it is something you cannot change, then what must you do to choose contentment?

214

14

The Legend of Montana Slim

———————•———————

Three seasoned wilderness adventurers—Loco Pete, Jack-knife Willie, and Montana Slim—stumbled upon the old map together while prospecting. The map revealed the location of buried treasure, hidden beneath an abandoned cabin in remote, dangerous terrain beyond the big mountain. It would be a difficult journey but well worth the effort. The long-lost treasure contained enough gold and silver for five lifetimes of opulence. And it was there for the taking.

But there would be no splitting the treasure between these three rivals. Winner take all—that was the rule of the wilderness. First one to reach the cache lived in luxury for life. The also-rans lived only to search again. To be fair, the treasure seekers agreed not to leave before dawn. As darkness fell, they settled into their respective shelters to plot strategies for the journey.

There were only two ways to reach the treasure: *over* the mountain or *around* the mountain. For Loco Pete, it was a no-brainer. The mountain route might be more direct, but it was too cold up there and the climb too strenuous. Going around the mountain would take longer, but it was easier and more enjoyable. He'd have plenty of food and water, and the temperature would be moderate. No cliffs, crags, or crevasses, no chilly thin air to tax the lungs. Why risk a fall or a blizzard when you could enjoy a leisurely stroll through the valley?

Montana Slim was just as firmly convinced to take the more direct route over the mountain. It would be a more arduous journey, full of risk and danger. But Slim, like the others, was tough and experienced, able to handle the mountain's challenge. And the elevation should keep him above the storms that moved through the lowlands each afternoon. Besides, every step over the mountain would take Slim one step closer to the treasure. And there was nothing more important to Montana Slim than capturing that prize.

Jackknife Willie thought such an important quest required deep reflection and extensive planning. For this adventurer, that meant getting a good night's sleep and waking up refreshed to consider the options. So Willie snuffed out his fire early and crawled into his bedroll.

At daybreak, Loco Pete and Montana Slim loaded their packs in silence and set out. Just a few hundred feet from camp the trail diverged. Slim took the fork heading for the mountain looming on the horizon, and Pete turned toward the valley. Each noted the other's choice with surprise as the distance between them quickly expanded. Soon they could no longer see each other, and the race was on.

Jackknife Willie awakened two hours later and lay there for another hour thinking about all the wonderful things the treasure could buy. He couldn't understand why Loco Pete and Montana Slim would leave before breakfast.

Loco Pete strolled across the foothill meadow at a leisurely pace. Creeks and ponds along the way were numerous, so the hiker drank when thirsty and stopped often to refill his canteen. Low-hanging fruit was also a welcome change from stale rations, so there was plenty to eat en route and to stash away for later. Afternoon heat in the lowlands caused Loco Pete to slow the pace and seek the trees for shade. Then a dark thunderstorm rolled through the valley, turning parts of the trail into a bog and requiring some detours. But as night fell, Loco Pete made camp, confident that the long way around was definitely the more enjoyable route.

Soon after leaving Loco Pete, Montana Slim began the long, steep ascent of the mountain. The stark, early-morning chill kept the climber moving steadily just to stay warm. Slim ascended as quickly as caution and efficiency would allow, selecting footholds and handholds with precision and care, staying as close to a direct line to his goal as possible. The thinner, cooler air required fewer stops for rest and water, which Slim rationed carefully. From this elevation, Slim watched the thunderstorm sweep through the valley below while the afternoon sun drenched the mountainside with pleasant warmth. The climber was able to continue the ascent long after sunset before retiring in a small cave. Slim expected to crest the mountain tomorrow afternoon and have the distant goal in sight during the long descent.

After a big breakfast, Jackknife Willie unpacked and repacked his gear several times, trying to decide if he should leave anything behind in order to travel faster. When the afternoon storm blew in, Willie decided it would be better to stay put for the night and set out in the morning—unless something else came up.

Another brief storm in the night left the lowland terrain damp and dusted the mountaintop with snow. The inclement weather kept Jackknife Willie in camp another day. The two others were slowed but not stopped by the elements. Loco Pete laughed at the thought of Slim trapped in the snow above. He wandered off the trail to visit an old prospector friend in the gulch. Meanwhile, Montana Slim skirted much of the snowfall by staying to the leeward side of the upward slope. Eating and drinking sparingly, Slim maintained a rigorous but safe pace toward the summit.

By afternoon, Loco Pete was into the rolling foothills and nearing the "corner" of the mountain. In a couple of hours he would stroll around the corner and head in the general direction of the treasure's location. At the same time, Montana Slim had crested the summit and left the snow behind on a cautious but hasty descent. From this vantage point, Slim could make out landmarks on the valley floor that pointed the way to the cabin and revealed obstacles to be avoided. It was better than looking at the treasure map.

Montana Slim camped in the foothills that night and set out early on a straight course to the cabin, hoping to arrive before nightfall. He was too focused on landmarks to look for Loco Pete or Jackknife Willie. Slim had aimed every possible step of the journey toward the location of the treasure. He had ignored the ease and distractions of the lowlands and risked the dangers of the mountain, believing it provided a clear vision and direct route to the prize.

At the end of the second day, Jackknife Willie's pack was finally ready to go. But he would need at least another half day in camp to evaluate the different approaches to the cabin. Perhaps there was a third way the others had not considered. Willie would give it some careful thought tomorrow.

Loco Pete struck out early on the third day, ready for another pleasant day of hiking and the prospect of finding the treasure. With the mountain now behind him, all he had to do was amble in the general direction of the cabin and he would likely stumble upon it. But the map had not accounted for a rock slide and a swollen stream, which took Pete off course.

It was near midnight by the time Pete finally found the rundown cabin, which was dark and deserted. The walk in the woods had been pleasant, and now he would be rich beyond his wildest dreams. Striking a match, Pete pulled up the floorboard, ready to unearth the riches. Instead he found an empty pit in the earth and a quickly scrawled note. It read:

Loco Pete and Jackknife Willie,

You lost the treasure before you left camp. If you want to reach a goal, you must do whatever it takes to stay headed in that direction. Every action has a consequence.

Farewell,

Montana Slim

Where Do You Want to Go?

As wise—and now very wealthy—Montana Slim said, every action has a consequence. It is important to evaluate every step you take in life, because each one takes you in a certain direction. Do you know where you want to go? You may have a goal in mind—a great treasure, perhaps the true personal wealth we have been discussing. Are you vectoring today—right this minute as you read these words—to hit that target? Or are you, like Loco Pete, wandering off in a different direction, perhaps on a seemingly easier or more pleasant path, hoping it will get you where you want to go? Worse yet, are you hunkered down in camp like Jackknife Willie, mired in the "paralysis of analysis" over which step to take?

Two things must happen if you want to find the "treasure" I have been talking about in this book. First, you must be clear about where you want to go. As best-selling author Stephen Covey says, you must "begin with the end in mind." At this point, I have a good idea about the end you have in mind. You probably would have tossed this book aside long ago unless you welcomed the concept that the rewards of true personal wealth are found on the path of influence. You're still here, so am I right in assuming that you are ready to make true personal wealth your goal?

That's half the battle—committing to a goal. And I think you have made a great choice. Just for the record, here are some of the important elements of true personal wealth you are aiming for.

- You desire to accumulate and profitably manage capital in all the lifeWealth dimensions: financial, relational, physical, intellectual, and spiritual. You want to integrate and balance these facets of your life for maximum productivity and enjoyment.
- You intend to capitalize on all life experiences—good and bad—and "bank" them in your experience portfolio for future use and profit.
- You are committed to maximizing your life experiences and lifeWealth capital through all three phases

220

of life—foundation, framework, finish—and leaving a rich legacy for all who know you.

- You reject an existence-centered or self-centered life, choosing instead an others-centered life. Put another way, you have determined to minimize your steps on paths of indifference or indulgence in order to focus your energies on the path of influence.

- You have chosen to make a vector change, setting a course for influence and true personal wealth.

- You intend to focus your life purpose and passions into a clear vision for your life. You further intend to live purposefully to fulfill that vision and realize true personal wealth.

- You are committed to utilizing the resources at your disposal in order to experience growing success as you live out your vision.

- You desire your journey to be marked by uncommon generosity toward others. You intend to make a plan, work the plan, enjoy the victories, and learn from the setbacks. Your focus is on progress, not perfection.

Do these statements summarize for you the "treasure" you are out to win? Then you have a good idea where you want to go. In Covey's words, you have the end in mind. In fact, you not only have the end in mind, you have a good grasp of the path that will get you there. The second critical element is to begin the journey.

How Will You Get There?

Jackknife Willie never got his act together. By deciding to loll around camp, this so-called adventurer kissed good-bye any chance to win the treasure. In light of the great treasure to be won, Willie's lethargy was pathetic. Did you find yourself thinking, *Why doesn't he get moving? How stupid can he be?* Yet countless numbers of people are no closer to realizing their vision today than they were one, five, or ten years ago because, like Jackknife Willie, they just won't get off the dime and get going.

Jackknife Willie's ludicrous response to the opportunity at hand reminds us that we will never fulfill our vision and acquire true personal wealth by just sitting around dreaming and scheming, wishing and hoping, whining and moping. At some point you have to break camp and head out on the journey. In the words of wise King Solomon, "Lazy hands make a man poor, but diligent hands bring wealth."[1] If you don't get on the road and busy yourself with the task of living out your vision, you will never enjoy the rewards of true personal wealth.

Loco Pete and Montana Slim represent those who lock on to the goal and set out to achieve it. But the vital difference between these two adventurers ultimately determined who took home the treasure. Slim set out to take the more direct line to the treasure no matter what it cost him; Loco Pete was more interested in the pleasures of the journey, even though they diverted him from his ultimate destination. And as Slim said in his note, Loco Pete lost the treasure before he even left camp because he vectored too far in the wrong direction. Slim became rich because his steps were aimed in the direction of the prize. Your first steps from this point will reveal much about the success of your journey ahead.

First Steps

I challenge you to adopt the attitude, vision, and drive of someone like Montana Slim. For starters, I invite you

222

to take five "first steps" in the direction of true personal wealth during the coming week. Some of the steps you choose may overlap important, long-term decisions you have considered as you worked through the questions in the previous five chapters. But the first steps you select now will get you going in the right direction immediately.

In each of the five sections below, you will find a number of practical ways to invest your lifeWealth capital. Select one idea—or come up with an idea of your own—from each dimension. Then follow through with these others-centered acts at least once over the next seven days, not out of duty but in order to vector your thoughts, attitudes, and actions onto the path of influence. Don't select actions you are already doing; branch out and try something new. You may want to continue this process in the future, selecting and completing a few assignments each week. Experiencing these first steps will help you focus your vision for investing in others over the long haul.

Financial first steps. Select one way you will invest your finances and/or material resources in others this week.

☐ Leave more generous gratuities than usual for those who serve you.

☐ Treat a coworker or friend to lunch or dinner out.

☐ Donate a box of your clothing to a shelter for the homeless.

☐ Purchase a "just because I love you" gift for your spouse.

☐ Make a one-time donation to a worthy charity you have not supported.

☐ Increase your contribution to your church.

☐ Support a fund-raiser for a worthy cause.

☐ Open a secret savings account for your grandchild with your own money.

Relational first steps. Here are several suggested ways for investing yourself in your relationships. Select one to put into practice.

☐ Take your child on a "date" and make sure he or she has a good time.

☐ Telephone a loved one you haven't talked with in a while just to ask how he or she is doing.

☐ Make a date to sit down with your spouse and ask about his or her dreams and desires for the next year.

☐ Select one person each day to affirm verbally.

☐ Send an encouraging e-mail to a discouraged friend or coworker.

☐ Spend an afternoon visiting lonely patients in a hospital or nursing home.

☐ Think of questions you can use in conversation to focus on others and draw them out.

Physical first steps. Which of the following suggestions would help you invest yourself in the health and recreation of others?

☐ Take your family on an after-dinner walk.

☐ Spend an evening with your family discussing ideas for vacation.

☐ Teach your children how to interpret the "nutrition facts" printed on packaged foods.

☐ Volunteer to perform a physically taxing task for someone: ironing, lifting, carrying, or repairing, for example.

☐ Host a game night for your child and his or her friends.

☐ Volunteer four hours to your church for whatever tasks need to be done.

☐ Watch a favorite TV program with your child and discuss the positive and negative influences.

Intellectual first steps. Here are several ways you can invest your skills and abilities in others:

☐ Teach your child how to balance a checkbook.

☐ Teach your child the correct way to do a household chore, not just showing how it's done but coaching and working alongside the child.

☐ If applicable, donate your knowledge and expertise to your church or another not-for-profit organization.

☐ Offer to spend extra time helping a new coworker learn tasks, equipment, or protocol.

☐ Teach your children a skill you learned from your parents when you were a child.

☐ Sign up for a class that will further help you develop your special skills and abilities to serve others.

Spiritual first steps. Remember: We invest ourselves in God not for his benefit but for ours. Here are a few suggestions to consider:

☐ Read something from the Bible every day.

☐ Begin each morning by asking God to direct your steps.

☐ Ask a minister or Christian friend to recommend good books about getting to know God better. Read one of the books suggested.

☐ Ask a friend to share with you how he or she came to believe in God.

☐ Take a moment before each meal to thank God for meeting your needs and to ask him to strengthen you to serve him and others.

☐ Say prayers with your children at bedtime.

☐ Sign up for a Bible study group appropriate to your knowledge of the Bible.

When we consider the Legend of Montana Slim, the analogy for our lives breaks down in a hurry, of course. You are not in a winner-take-all contest to acquire true personal wealth. In fact, you are not in competition with anyone; each of us has the same golden opportunity to enjoy the fulfillment and satisfaction of an others-centered life. But how you decide to get there has everything to do with how fully you will enjoy the rewards of such a life. Are you content to take the easy way around, to invest in others when it is convenient or profitable to you? Or will you take the high road by vectoring your life directly at the goal and making every step count?

Indifference, Indulgence, or Influence?

We all must choose which path we will take on our journey through life. Once we choose, then the journey begins. It may seem slow. It may seem as if we are making little progress. We may not ever know entirely how successful we were in traveling our path. But our choice will determine how we live this life, enjoy this life, finish, and leave this life. The choice is yours. It is time to decide.

226

Small Change *Challenges*

- "Every action has a consequence!" Complete the "First Steps" section in this chapter.
- Take action. Vector your life directly at the goal and make every step count!

Questions for Consideration or Discussion

---•---

Chapter 1

1. Are you satisfied with the direction your life is taking you?
2. Do you have a clear picture of where you want to go?
3. Do you find yourself confused or frustrated trying to stay on track?
4. What vector change could you make right now to move you closer to your desired destination?
5. In what area of your life do you find it necessary to make consistent vector changes?

Chapter 2

1. How would you define success?
2. Which of the hallmarks of success in our culture (power, fame, prestige, achievement, possessions) tempt you the most in your pursuit of success?

3. How has "Affluenza" impacted you and your family?
4. How does Benjamin Mays's quote impact you?

> The tragedy of life doesn't lie in not reaching your goal. The tragedy lies in having no goal to reach. It isn't a calamity to die with dreams unfulfilled, but it is a calamity not to dream. . . . It is not a disgrace not to reach the stars, but it is a disgrace to have no stars to reach for. Not failure but low aim is sin.

Chapter 3

1. In what ways do you find yourself living a *"disintegrating life"*?
2. What area of your life seems to be requiring a disproportionate amount of your time?
3. Look at the comparison of an "Integrating" vs. "Disintegrating" life on page 46. Circle the appropriate description in each area that represents your life.
4. As you imagined yourself vectoring toward a life of success and integration, what did that image look like for you? What vector changes need to be made right now to move you toward that outcome?

Chapter 4

1. How would you finish the statement *"Wealthy is the person who . . ."*?
2. For each of the five dimensions of wealth, write a brief description of the wealth you have accumulated.
3. Set aside some time in which you can think about your past from your first memory to today. Make a list of the events you consider to be significant, both good and bad. Just start writing and don't think about

it too much. Once you have your list, which ten events would you consider the most significant in terms of impact on your life?

4. As you look at each of those ten events, what wisdom, insight or knowledge did you gain from those experiences?

5. Look at the exercise described on page 65. As you imagine yourself at the end of your life looking back with contentment and satisfaction, what did your life look like? Describe what meant the most in each of the dimensions of wealth. What vector changes should you make right now to move you toward that kind of outcome?

Chapter 5

1. When you look at your foundation phase, what deposits were made in your experience portfolio on your behalf by others in your life?

2. As you look back on your life, is there any experience that you need to revisit in order to recapture equity in your experience portfolio?

3. Whether you are currently retired or working toward that end, how do you define or describe retirement?

4. What is your response to the Howard Hendricks quote: *"The day your past is more exciting than your future is the day you begin to die"*?

5. In two or three sentences, what will people say about you when you die?

Chapter 6

1. In what ways do you find yourself venturing down the path of indifference?

2. In what ways do you find yourself tempted to pursue the path of indulgence?
3. In each of the five dimensions of wealth, how are you following the path of influence?
4. Make a list of all the spheres of influence in which you find yourself (family, friends, work, church, community groups, professional groups, neighborhood, and so on).
5. Which of these areas of your life offers the greatest opportunity for influence?
6. In which spheres of influence *must* you win?

Chapter 7

1. What small vector changes or choices that you made in the past have caused significant impact, good or bad?
2. What kind of vector changes could you make today that could create a "domino effect" or "trickle-down influence"?
3. On page 119 I discussed the idea of creating a "150-year legacy." Think about this concept in your life. Describe the legacy you could create.
4. The most recent life expectancy calculation is seventy-one years for men and seventy-eight years for women. With that in mind, estimate the number of days you might have left on this earth. How does that change your thinking in terms of intentional vector changes?
5. What is the single most important vector change you want to make right now to create lasting influence?

Chapter 8

1. On a scale of 1 to 10, how committed are you to acting on the lifeFocus paradigm?

2. Who are the most important people in your life who need to be part of your team?
3. How do distractions and procrastination interfere with your progress down the path of influence?
4. What keeps you from taking action on important issues in life?

Chapter 9

1. What is the "one thing" in your box that would best describe your purpose?
2. How does your "one thing" influence the financial, relational, physical, intellectual, and spiritual aspects of your life?
3. If you had to give all of your material possessions to someone or to some organization other than your family, who would you choose?
4. What causes you to pound the table with emotion or pace the floor with endless energy when you talk about it?

Chapter 10

1. What do you think are your unique abilities?
2. In what ways do you find yourself living "reactively" in each of the dimensions of wealth?
3. What proactive steps could you take in each of the dimensions of wealth?
4. Write down three strategies for accomplishing your goals.

Chapter 11

1. What steps should you consider to be more prepared for the opportunities that come your way?

2. What new skill or interest would you like to develop?
3. How would you prioritize all the roles and responsibilities you have in life?
4. In terms of time spent, how do these activities stack up?
5. If there is a difference between your priorities and how you spend your time, is this a result of a "season" of life? If not, what changes need to happen?

Chapter 12

1. List some specific ways you could give some of your time, talent, treasure, and touch to others.
2. If someone were to examine your checkbook, what would they find?
3. What small vector changes could you make with regard to your generosity in each of the dimensions of wealth?
4. In what sphere of influence could you begin to mentor someone younger than you?
5. What is the first step you should make toward a mentoring relationship?

Chapter 13

1. How have your imperfections and shortcomings prevented you from experiencing contentment?
2. Where are you vulnerable in terms of not being content?
3. How could you exercise contentment in each of the dimensions of wealth?
4. How much influence do the media and cultural expectations have in breeding discontent in your life?

Chapter 14

1. Which of the three adventurers do you most live like?
2. In what ways do you demonstrate any of the qualities of each of the adventurers?
3. Do you have a clear picture of where you are going in life?
4. What are the first steps you must take in each of the dimensions of wealth that will move you toward your dreams and goals?

Notes

———————————•———————————

Chapter 2: How Do You Define Success?

1. *Merriam-Webster's Collegiate Dictionary*, 10th ed., s.v. "affluence."
2. Robert Greene, *The 48 Laws of Power* (New York: Penguin USA, 2000), ix–xiv.
3. Alfie Kohn, "In Pursuit of Affluence, at a High Price," *The New York Times on the Web*, February 2, 1999, www.nytimes.com.
4. Ibid.
5. John De Graaf, David Wann, and Thomas H. Naylor, *Affluenza: The All-Consuming Epidemic* (San Francisco: Berrett-Koehler Publishers, 2001), 1–2.
6. Ibid., 4.
7. John Cook, comp., *The Book of Positive Quotations* (Minneapolis, Minn.: Fairview Press, 1997), 65.
8. Ibid., 351.
9. *The Oxford Dictionary of Quotations*, (Oxford: Oxford University Press, 2001), 432.
10. *Book of Positive Quotations*, 110.
11. Matthew 16:24–25 NLT.
12. *Book of Positive Quotations*, 358.

Chapter 3: Are You Holding It All Together?

1. Michael Moschen, quoted in Thomas Addington and Stephen Graves, "Juggling Life," *Life@Work Journal* 3, no. 6 (November/December 2000): 42.
2. Ibid.
3. Addington and Graves, "Juggling Life," 42.

4. Adapted from Moschen, in Addington and Graves, "Juggling Life," 42–47.

Chapter 4: A Life Rich with Experiences

1. Ecclesiastes 7:14.
2. See Genesis 37–50.
3. Genesis 50:20.
4. Author unknown, 6 March 2002, http://www.fbc-covington.org/pastor/lifelines03_06_2002.htm, accessed 3 December 2003.
5. Proverbs 17:16.

Chapter 5: An Overview of Your Life

1. Proverbs 16:31.
2. Howard Hendricks, speech to the FamilyLife speaker team, St. Petersburg, Florida, January 2001.

Chapter 6: The Road to True Personal Wealth

1. Author unknown, http://toddlerstoday.com/resources/articles/creed.htm, accessed 3 December 2003.
2. John Wooden, *"An Interview with Coach John Wooden on the Qualities All Achievers Share,"* interview by Anthony Robbins, Robbins Research International, Inc., 1999.
3. 2 Corinthians 9:7.
4. 2 Timothy 2:2.

Chapter 7: The Vector Principle

1. Michael Janke, "Generational Discipline," http://self-discipline.8m.com/generational_discipline.htm, accessed 29 November 2003.
2. Ibid.
3. Psalm 90:12 KJV.

Chapter 8: Now What?

1. Proverbs 6:9–11 NLT.

Chapter 9: Focus Your Vision

1. Author unknown, "Keeping Your Goals in Sight," adapted from Jack Canfield and Mark Victor Hansen, eds., *A Second Helping of Chicken Soup for the Soul* (Boca Raton, Fla.: Health Communications, 1995), 237.
2. Proverbs 29:18 KJV.

3. Canfield and Hansen, eds., *Second Helping of Chicken Soup*, 237.
4. *City Slickers*, prod. Irby Smith, dir. Ron Underwood, 1 hr. 54 min., Castle Rock Entertainment, 1991, videocassette.
5. Bob Buford, *Half Time* (Grand Rapids: Zondervan, 1995), 49–50.
6. Matthew 22:37–38.

Chapter 10: Live Purposefully

1. Samuel Butler, *Notebooks* (1951, 151), quoted in Robert Andrews, comp., *The Columbia Dictionary of Quotations*, (New York: Columbia University Press, 1993), 301.
2. *Book of Positive Quotations*, 540.
3. Joshua 1:6–9.

Chapter 11: Equip for Success

1. Matthew 25:1–13 NLT.
2. Michael J. Gelb, *How to Think Like Leonardo da Vinci: Seven Steps to Genius Every Day* (New York: Delacorte Press, 1998), 68.
3. Patrick Henry, in a speech to the Second Virginia Convention, March 23, 1775, quoted in Caroline Kennedy, *A Patriot's Handbook* (New York: Hyperion, 2003), 398.
4. *Book of Positive Quotations*, 518.
5. Proverbs 27:17 NLT

Chapter 12: Give from the Heart

1. Kenneth H. Blanchard and S. Truett Cathy, *The Generosity Factor* (Grand Rapids: Zondervan, 2002), 50–51.
2. Acts 20:35.
3. Luke 6:38 NLT.
4. Mark 12:41–44 NLT.
5. Matthew 6:21.
6. Psalm 46:10.

Chapter 13: Enjoy the Journey

1. See Acts 9:1–9.
2. Philippians 4:11–13.
3. 2 Corinthians 9:8.
4. 1 Timothy 6:7–10.
5. 1 Corinthians 12:15–19.
6. 1 Corinthians 12:20–25.

Chapter 14: The Legend of Montana Slim

1. Proverbs 10:4.

Jerry Foster is the CEO and founder of Foster Group, a company committed to assisting its clients with life coaching and financial management since 1989. Jerry Foster has been listed in *WORTH* magazine as one of the top financial planners in America, and *Medical Economics* lists him as one of the top 150 financial planners in the country.

Jerry is on the speaker team for CrossTrainers, which is a group of over five hundred men meeting weekly in the Des Moines area. This group's purpose is to equip men to be effective husbands, fathers, employers, and employees as well as public servants.

Jerry and his wife, Nancy, are speakers with FamilyLife Weekend to Remember Marriage Conferences. Jerry also speaks throughout the nation on financial planning and life coaching and has been a contributor to several magazines on these issues as well.

Jerry and Nancy have been married for twenty-five years and have four children. They make their home in Adel, Iowa.